T0316659

Cambridge Elements ≡

Elements in Politics and Society in Southeast Asia
edited by
Edward Aspinall
Australian National University
Meredith L. Weiss
University at Albany, SUNY

RITUAL AND REGION

The Invention of ASEAN

Mathew Davies
Australian National University, Canberra

CAMBRIDGE
UNIVERSITY PRESS

CAMBRIDGE
UNIVERSITY PRESS

University Printing House, Cambridge CB2 8BS, United Kingdom

One Liberty Plaza, 20th Floor, New York, NY 10006, USA

477 Williamstown Road, Port Melbourne, VIC 3207, Australia

314–321, 3rd Floor, Plot 3, Splendor Forum, Jasola District Centre,
New Delhi – 110025, India

79 Anson Road, #06–04/06, Singapore 079906

Cambridge University Press is part of the University of Cambridge.

It furthers the University's mission by disseminating knowledge in the pursuit of
education, learning, and research at the highest international levels of excellence.

www.cambridge.org
Information on this title: www.cambridge.org/9781108457965
DOI: 10.1017/9781108686785

First published 2018

A catalogue record for this publication is available from the British Library.

ISBN 978-1-108-45796-5 Paperback
ISSN 2515-2998 (online)
ISSN 2515-298X (print)

Ritual and Region

The Invention of ASEAN

Elements in Politics and Society in Southeast Asia

DOI: 10.1017/9781108686785
First published online: September 2018

Mathew Davies
Australian National University, Canberra

Abstract: Why has ASEAN endured and why do members, many of whom remain comparatively weak and poor, continue to invest in the regional project? Existing answers, either that ASEAN is meaningless or that it has transformed regional affairs through the creation of shared values, are both misplaced. Neither argument is empirically plausible. Instead, this work argues that ASEAN has and continues to serve state interest through the creation of a shared ritual and symbolic framework. This framework has mitigated regional tension through the performance of regionalism, but has not fundamentally addressed the sources of that tension.

Keywords: ASEAN, Regionalism, Southeast Asia, International Organisation

Isbns: 9781108457965 (PB) 9781108686785 (OC)
Issns: 2515-2998 (online), 2515-298X (print)

Contents

ASEAN has fascinated and perplexed me since I started my doctoral studies some fifteen years ago. It is easy to be sceptical of ASEAN, and for quite a few years I embraced that scepticism. The diversities of the region are well-known, and this has led to ten members with very different goals and interests, all of which serve to fray the regional project. Even the most notable trait of the region – the absence of major inter-state war between its members – has a chimerical quality to it, and the more one looks, the harder it is to attribute this 'peace' to ASEAN in any convincing way. Yet regional elites continue to take ASEAN seriously despite its failings. They invest considerable time and resources into its running and, despite its travails, whether in the South China Sea or the realisation of its internal goals, there is as yet little evidence of members disengaging with it. This continued interest displayed by the intelligent and politically savvy leaders of the region caught my attention. Whilst my scepticism has not been washed away, I am more open to the possibility that ASEAN's value is more than a list of its clear accomplishments would suggest.

This work, then, is part of my effort to appreciate why ASEAN continues to be important to regional elites. In doing so I seek neither to defend the regional project nor to condemn it. Instead I wish to make a small contribution to understanding it – one that takes the actions and words of practitioners seriously, although not necessarily at face value. Rituals and symbols are presented here as a way to understand the endurance and continued value attached to the regional project. I emphasise some things that others take for granted – the coming together of leaders, diplomats, and experts, and the orchestration and presentation of those meetings in both visual and written mediums. The rhythm and texture of regionalism as a practice interests me in this work.

This focus, I hope, holds the scepticism and optimism about ASEAN in balance in a way that respects the history and politics of the region. It allows me to argue that ASEAN has made a contribution to regional peace and security, just not in the way that its most ardent supporters claim. It also allows me to capture the dualism of ASEAN, its expanding activities and failings, in a new light; the creation and repetition of ambitious goals without reference to a failure to achieve these goals becomes central to the performance of ASEAN, not evidence of its weakness.

Finally, this work should be read as part of an ongoing conversation of my own thinking about the region. Too often existing frameworks from my own discipline, International Relations, have misunderstood ASEAN and framed it as either largely irrelevant or incredibly powerful. The wealth of empirical evidence for both sides of this debate suggests they are equally off the mark. Yet something holds the region together, both animating and shaping its politics and contributing to its successes and failures. Whatever this 'something' is, we should seek to articulate and understand it clearly, honestly, and sensitively. This work is my attempt to do just that.

1 Introduction

In November 2015, the Secretariat of the Association of Southeast Asian Nations (ASEAN) released a sixty-eight page document to which no one beyond ASEAN paid any attention. The *Guide to ASEAN Practices and Protocol* is meticulous, detailing every aspect of how ASEAN organises its events. For ASEAN Summits, there are rules about the stage setting, the backdrops used, the flags to be displayed, and the seating of heads of state and government, spouses, mere VIPs, very VIPs, and ministers. Different seating arrangements are specified for ASEAN Summit plenary meetings, ASEAN Summit retreat meetings, signing ceremonies, and luncheon meetings. Similar levels of detail are provided for various ASEAN+1 meetings, ASEAN+3 (China, Japan, and South Korea) meetings, the East Asia Summit, advisory councils, gala dinners, hand-over ceremonies, closing ceremonies, and press conferences. Rules are outlined for meetings at ministerial and senior-official levels, and again for meetings with external partners (ASEAN 2015). The *Guide* is a blueprint for the management of ASEAN's stagecraft; how ASEAN presents itself to its members, how those members present themselves to one another under the ASEAN banner, and how the world sees the organisation.

It is easy to dismiss the *Guide* as a meaningless document produced at the expense of tackling other more important issues, and as yet another example of ASEAN's fixation on process. How can it possibly matter who stands where, given the range of internal and external challenges that ASEAN faces? Yet, to dismiss the *Guide* as not meaningful, and as not offering insight into what makes regionalism work in Southeast Asia, is a mistake. The *Guide* reveals the importance of two things that are rarely spoken about in the context of ASEAN – rituals and symbols. Rituals and symbols serve as a *representation* of a region at peace to citizens, other member-states, and the wider international community. However, this representation is not supported by the empirical record, which shows evidence of suspicion, mistrust, and competition. Rituals help to bracket this suspicion, and so the reality of the situation has mattered less than would be thought. Rituals and symbols also serve as a mechanism for the *performance* of regionalism where a wider circle of elites, and even individual citizens, engage in activities that demonstrate ASEAN's harmony as if there were no tension between them.

Rituals and symbols have become the way that ASEAN creates the impression of unity in the absence of other unifiers. In this work I argue that ASEAN has fostered a form of regional order predicated on rituals and symbols. This order prioritises coexistence, national freedoms (from interference and to interfere), and 'opt-in' cooperation at the regional level – rituals and symbols promote and protect these goals not by addressing the root causes of threats to stability, but by limiting the potential damage that these threats can cause. As such, rituals and symbols have helped keep in check the centrifugal tendencies of the region, ensuring the continuation of ASEAN.

In this section, I introduce ASEAN by highlighting three defining features of its approach to regional governance. I then present the academic debate about ASEAN and regional order, framing it as a struggle to define what ASEAN is, why it endures, and whether it is successful. Whilst illuminating, this debate is enduring because each side is characterised by prominent and inescapable empirical weaknesses. Rituals and symbols offer a way to address these weaknesses. I outline the meaning of these terms and what they suggest about the creation and management of order, and then apply that to ASEAN.

1.1 The Three Characteristics of ASEAN

Formed in 1967, ASEAN is perhaps the most successful regional organisation outside the European Union. It has endured the Cold War and its ending, the 1997 Asian financial crisis, significant political change within many member-states, expansion of its membership from five to ten, and, at least so far, the rise of China.[1] To orient the reader and allow for the coming argument, I highlight three defining features of ASEAN – the preoccupation with sovereignty, the nature of regional reform over the last fifty years, and the issue of non-compliance. Understanding these three characteristics provides a perspective on the nature of ASEAN's regional order.

1.1.1 Sovereignty

ASEAN was created for the single purpose of promoting the enjoyment of national sovereignty by its members. Throughout most of ASEAN's history, this has served as a metaphor for promoting the freedom of authoritarian elites to go about their business unencumbered by internal and external challenges. This was not surprising given the situation in Southeast Asia in the 1960s.

---

[1] The original five members were Indonesia, Malaysia, the Philippines, Singapore, and Thailand. Brunei joined in 1984, Vietnam in 1995, Laos and Myanmar in 1997, and Cambodia in 1999. The latter four members are known as the CLMV (Cambodia, Laos, Myanmar, and Vietnam) countries.

The very diverse states of the region had a shared recent history; all (except Thailand) had been colonised by European powers, and many had experienced occupation by the Japanese during the Second World War, decolonisation, weak central governments, the challenge of communist insurgencies, geopolitical competition between superpowers, and fear of a return to subservience to Western states. Elites were in conflict with each other over borders and ruled, often nominally, over societies rife with poverty and human insecurity. The regional project in Southeast Asia was to address these concerns and, in doing so, make states more, not less, sovereign in name and practice. ASEAN termed this as a commitment to building national and regional resilience 'on the principles of self-confidence, self-reliance, mutual respect, cooperation and solidarity' (ASEAN 1976c: article 12).

The commitment to sovereignty is not unique to ASEAN; it is shared by many other regional organisations.[2] However, none have taken it as seriously as ASEAN. Commitments to sovereignty have been ASEAN's constant companion from its founding 1967 Bangkok Treaty, to the dual agreements of 1976 (the Bali I Accords comprising the Treaty of Amity and Cooperation (TAC) and the Declaration of ASEAN Concord), to the 2007 ASEAN Charter. ASEAN's preoccupation with sovereignty has resulted in a diplomatic environment shaped to respect and promote the sovereign prerogatives of its members. At a formal level, the commitments have been embodied in documents and treaties; ASEAN has stringent commitments to procedural equality. From these formal commitments, the 'ASEAN way' has emerged, which has attracted considerable attention. Although there remains ambiguity about what precisely it is, Acharya (1997: 328) argues that the 'ASEAN way' at its core 'consists of a code of conduct for inter-state behaviour as well as a decision-making process based on consultations and consensus' (Acharya 1997: 328). In this vein, some have linked this regional code to local Malay cultural practices of *musyawarah* and *mufakat* in an effort to identify the roots of this approach (Nischalke 2000: 90). The 'ASEAN way' has been framed as an indigenous alternative to Western-style conflict resolution (Möller 1998: 1088). Together, the commitments to sovereignty and the formal and informal procedural framework of ASEAN give the impression of a strong defence of sovereignty through realising two key aspects – non-intervention (not engaging in activities within another state's territory) and non-interference (not commenting on activities within another state).

---

[2] For example, the Charter of the Organization of American States calls on members 'to defend their sovereignty' (article 1), and the Constitutive Act of the African Union frames the objective of the organisation as to 'defend the sovereignty, territorial integrity and independence of its Member States' (article 3b).

1.1.2 Regional Reform

The commitment to sovereignty throughout ASEAN's history does not mean that ASEAN has not changed (Davies 2016) – reform has been a key part of ASEAN's story. ASEAN's first thirty years were characterised by a slow and steady expansion of activities as regional elites slowly fleshed out the vague commitments to economic growth, political cooperation, and social stability that were reached in Bangkok. The year 1997 marked a partial discontinuity in the history of ASEAN reform. Spurred on by the Asian financial crisis of 1997, regional elites expanded ASEAN's activities into previously off-limit areas such as democracy and human rights, whilst also developing further their existing commitments. Unsurprisingly, the development of ASEAN's commitments led to a more complex institutional environment. For much of its history, ASEAN has been famously 'lightweight', with few meetings, a small and weak secretariat, and very little bureaucratic capacity of its own. Yet since 1997, ASEAN has become more densely institutionalised. At every level, from heads of state down, there are now regular meetings, committees, and work groups, supported by a growing secretariat based in Jakarta. In comparison to an institution that held just a handful of meetings in 1967, there are now hundreds of scheduled events and, behind those, a rich and complex network of constant communication (ASEAN 2017a). Yet underpinning all these reforms has been the constant restatement of the sovereign rights of members, and 'on-paper' commitments to non-intervention and non-interference.

1.1.3 Non-compliance

The tension between the centrality of sovereignty and an expansive range of governance commitments has emphasised ASEAN's perennial shortcoming of a lack of compliance with its commitments. The same states that created these central regional commitments – particularly the apparent defence of sovereignty and resultant prohibitions on interference and intervention – have also never lived up to them. The history of Southeast Asia, before and after 1967, has been characterised by frequent interference and intervention in the domestic affairs of fellow-members. Perplexingly, these activities have not attracted much, if any, opprobrium from other states in the region, and instead are seemingly accepted as a routine occurrence in the life of the region. In Southeast Asia, respect for sovereignty is the most valorised of commitments and simultaneously one of the most violated. Outside these central commitments, today's ASEAN faces compliance shortfalls in many areas. In the promotion of human rights and democracy, and in issues as diverse as environmental protection, economic integration, and trade policy, ASEAN's commitments are routinely violated. This gap between declarations and reality is expanding, yet ASEAN members remain unperturbed by their commitments being violated with impunity. ASEAN's order is characterised not so much by consensus, but instead by carefully governed disagreement, both amongst members, and between members and the regional commitments they have created.

1.2 The Academic Debate about ASEAN

ASEAN's preoccupation with sovereignty, its expanding remit, and the gap between 'on-paper' commitments and reality reveal ASEAN's enigmatic nature. Why do states create commitments that they have no intention of living up to? Why do members continue to invest time and resources into a regional project that seems so slight? What *is* ASEAN given its track record, and is it a success?

The two leading strands of academic debate about ASEAN were memorably characterised by John Ravenhill (2009) as either ASEAN sceptics or ASEAN boosters (see also Eaton & Stubbs 2006). Sceptical arguments about ASEAN are largely rooted in the realist tradition of International Relations (IR), with its focus on state power, self-interest, and mutual suspicion. Michael Leifer was a key figure in this debate (Leifer 1974; Emmerson 2006). Scepticism about ASEAN today can be characterised as a family of related claims rather than a single position. Some emphasise that contemporary ASEAN remains wedded to state sovereignty and state power, and therefore remains a captive of the ambitions and fears of national capitals (Narine 2009). This line of reasoning emphasises the commitments to sovereignty discussed above and the idea that since ASEAN is a vehicle of state power and freedom, it does not provide effective regional governance. ASEAN is seen as a weak institution, controlled entirely by its member-states who maintain a mutual suspicion of each other and of any commitments that would limit their freedoms. ASEAN's order is fragile and transitory, predicated on the whims of its most powerful members and, more importantly, of the global powers who play politics in Southeast Asia. This does not mean that ASEAN is useless, but it has little life beyond the utility that member-states see in it. At the most extreme end of the spectrum, the sceptical argument denies ASEAN's importance (Jones & Smith 2002, 2006).

The booster position is more positive about ASEAN, and has emerged over the last twenty years, led by Amitav Acharya (2001). The term 'security community', defined as a zone of peace where states share the reliable expectation of peaceful change, is crucial to the booster argument. Security communities produce reliable expectations of peace as states no longer think that armed conflict is an option in their interaction with other members of that community (the classic definition comes from Deutsch 1957). This 'unthinking' peace is the product of norms – inter-subjective beliefs about appropriate behaviour – and it is not surprising that booster arguments tend towards a constructivist framing of the region, emphasising the role of identity in international politics. In this reading, ASEAN is not just an institution created by states and beholden to them. Instead, ASEAN reveals the presence of deep social cooperation between member-states and their leaders, which in turn binds the region together in a thicker and fuller way than sceptics imagine is possible. ASEAN is not the captive of its member-states, and the member-states are not bound together by self-interest alone. Instead, a thick set of norms about appropriate behaviour and Southeast Asia's identity are commonly held across regional states. Central here are the diplomatic norms around consensus and unanimity, which, instead of signifying ASEAN's weakness, actually indicate its greatest achievement as they represent inter-subjective beliefs that create a true community. These shared norms bind members together and explain ASEAN's endurance and successes. In this sense, ASEAN's order is robust and enduring, resting as it does on a community of true sentiment shared at least by elites and spreading into the regional public.

Following Acharya's lead, Jürgen Haacke (2005) identified 'six norms' in ASEAN's diplomatic and security culture that comprised the 'ASEAN way' and mediated regional estrangement and insecurity.[3] Alice Ba (2009) focused on ideas about Southeast Asia to explain both regional troubles and unity, invoking constructivism to explore ideas about regional resilience. Hiro Katsumata (2004) traced shifting ASEAN diplomacy to new shared ideas about appropriate behaviour. Acharya (2004, 2005) continued to explore how shared ideas were shaping Southeast Asian regionalism, and was joined by others who focused on these ideas in different areas of ASEAN activity (Kraft 2001; Katsumata 2006; Collins 2007; Stubbs 2008).

The defining feature of the debate between these two frameworks is that both have generated non-replicable insights into ASEAN whilst at the same time never escaping their own serious explanatory shortcomings. Sceptical work explains why ASEAN is in so many ways a weak institution and why its

---

[3] The norms were 'sovereign equality; non-recourse to the use of force; non-interference and non-intervention; non-invocation of ASEAN to address unresolved bilateral conflict between members; quiet diplomacy; and mutual respect and tolerance'. See Haacke (2005: 214).

commitments are so often violated. And yet sceptical arguments are poorly suited to understanding how and why ASEAN has endured for more than fifty years in the face of such turbulent change, and why states, many of whom remain poor in material and social resources, continue to invest effort in ASEAN. If ASEAN does not do anything for its members, why do they bear the costs of the organisation? Why do they pursue more sophisticated regional commitments and processes when states have no intention of realising these commitments? Perhaps most importantly, how can sceptics explain the significant achievement of fifty years of regional peace? Inversely, the booster argument helps illuminate why states persist in bothering about ASEAN, why states wished to join the organisation in the 1990s, why peace has endured in Southeast Asia, and why ASEAN is central to Asia-Pacific regionalism. Yet boosters struggle to explain ASEAN's obvious limitations – if states are bound by these norms, why do they violate them so often, so openly, and with such impunity (Davies 2013a)? When looking at the reality of ASEAN member-states' practices of intervention against the presumed norm of non-intervention, Lee Jones (2012: 218) concludes that 'the constructivist understanding of norms is simply unsustainable'.[4]

Despite ASEAN's long history, and an expansive academic engagement with it, observers of Southeast Asian regionalism remain unsatisfied. Our leading frameworks are unable to grasp ASEAN's true nature – the boosters radically overstate their case whilst the sceptics radically understate theirs.[5] The argument that I present is intended to step between the optimism of the boosters and the negativity of the sceptics. I do not intend to replace many of the insights of these approaches so much as to situate them within a broader framework. Over its life, ASEAN has been buffeted by shifting power politics, changing notions of legitimacy, and the development of its members; each has a part to play in explaining the evolution and current form of regional governance. My claim that rituals and symbols provide a foundational account of ASEAN on top of which other arguments can be positioned and debated is modest. Rituals and symbols do not explain everything that has happened to ASEAN or that ASEAN has achieved. In the remainder of this section, I develop this new perspective on ASEAN. The sections that follow explore how this approach has developed, endured, and operated during ASEAN's existence.

---

[4] Jones's work is just one of many that question the 'real' nature of non-intervention. See also Narine (1997); Johnston (1999); Nischalke (2000).

[5] Parallels exist between the inapplicability of these frameworks and the claim that there is a mismatch between International Relations theory and the practice of non-Western actors. See discussion in Acharya (2011); Kim (2018).

1.3 Understanding Rituals and Symbols

The discipline of IR has dealt with rituals and symbols only sporadically.[6] In the study of IR in general and ASEAN in particular, rituals and symbols are mentioned but rarely investigated. Rituals have played a small role in the analysis of norms (Kratochwil 1989: 123–6) and in the study of peace-keeping (for example Rubinstein 2005: 536; Schirch 2005). The most sustained investigation has emerged from the study of diplomacy. The relationship between diplomacy, symbolism, and ritual is intrinsic in both Western (Neumann 2011) and non-Western traditions (Phillips 2017). Faizullaev (2013) emphasises the way that symbols represent the state and make it apparent to individuals, giving weight to their communicative, normative, and affective functions (see also Sending, Pouliot & Neumann 2015). Taku Yukawa (2017) refers to the 'ASEAN way' as a symbol of ASEAN but offers no conceptual analysis of this categorisation. Symbols have also been linked to the power of international organisations, especially the way in which they legitimate institutions and their functions (Hurd 2002, 2005; Chapman 2009). It is, however, in the fields of sociology and anthropology that much of the analytical investigation into rituals and symbols has occurred, and so it is these literatures that form the basis of the following discussion.

David Kertzer (1988: 6) provides what has become a standard definition for rituals and symbols. Rituals are defined as 'symbolic behavior that is socially standardized and repetitive' (Kertzer 1988: 9). Rituals provide some sort of organisation to social life, and a way to mesh together the regular and the improvised, the repetitive and the varying (Moore & Myerhoff 1977: 4, 5; Walzer 1967). Kertzer defines symbols as those things that 'instigate social action and define the individual's sense of self', which serve to make sense of the political process with which they are engaged. Rituals and symbols can only exercise importance because they are embodied and performed.[7] Moore and Myerhoff (1977: 6–7) note that rituals require repetition and formalisation, a public acting out of roles, special behavioural activities that exist only as part of the ritual, a clear order and sequence, an evocative presentational style including staging, and a clear

---

[6] There is also a small, now dated, literature that engages Emile Durkheim, whose work on the maintenance of societies provides much of the foundations of the study of rituals, and IR directly, although its focus is primarily on Kenneth Waltz's (mis)use of Durkheim's theory of mechanical and organic societies. See Larkins (1994).

[7] Fascinating parallels can be found between ASEAN's approach to performed ritualised regionalism and Clifford Geertz's (1980) pioneering work on Balinese society, in which he identified performance as the ends of political power, not a means to it.

collective dimension which binds together participants with each other and the audience with the ritual.[8]

The formalism of rituals is enhanced by the deployment of symbols in ceremonial contexts (Chase 2005: 115). Symbols are the content around which ritual action occurs – the national flag at the memorial ceremony, the mortarboard at an academic graduation, the ten ASEAN heads of state linking hands in front of a screen emblazoned with the ASEAN motto. Symbols imbue rituals with meaning. Symbols become tools for the 'meaningful objectification' of that which they represent, making that thing 'sensible' to participants and audience (Faizullaev 2013: 92). In turn this objectification serves to create bonds, motivate action, confer honour, legitimate authority, and shape political action (Cerulo 1995: 32–3).

Rituals do not emerge fully formed – instead, they are created and strengthened over time. In this sense there is a clear power dimension to the study of ritual (Kertzer 1988: 25; Charlesworth & Larking 2014: 8). The power of certain individuals helps create rituals (although not all rituals are consciously constituted), and the performance of rituals with a degree of social competence bestows power on others. Rituals articulate the authority of positions and practices beyond the individuals who for a short time perform these roles. Rituals help shape conversations about viable futures and retards heretical futures as unthinkable.

Creation, repetition, and performance indicate the presence of an important temporal dimension to the study of ritual, but rituals do more than simply emerge *over* time; they link participants and observers *to* time in a particular way. When engaging in ritual behaviour either as a participant or an observer, we are linked with the past and reassured in the present. In this way, the new and potentially objectionable is rendered traditional and conservative through ritual's emphasis on continuity. The past is the source of ritual behaviour, the validation of current practices, and the foundation of future thinking. It is widely accepted that rituals can vary in their fidelity to the reality of the material, social, and political worlds and can systematically misrepresent reality. Rituals can hide or reveal, delude or clarify (Kertzer 1988: 87). This opens up a gap between how something is represented and the reality of that thing being represented. In this way rituals help to veil and obscure disorder and its causes by giving the impression of timeless harmony and consensus, and represent a balance between cooperation and competition (Sennett 2013: 89).

---

[8] Oren and Solomon (2015: 317) similarly emphasise the significance of repetition in their discussion of ritualised incantation as a securitisation device.

The next step in understanding the value of an approach that emphasises rituals and symbols is to differentiate it from a constructivist framework as previously described. Realising a difference between a constructivist explanation and a ritual/symbol one (and so laying the groundwork for the greater explanatory power of the latter) requires that we examine the question of whether order is produced by shared meaning. Constructivists are engaged in a project to explore how beliefs shape political behaviour (Kaufmann & Pape 1999). At any given moment an agent possesses internalised beliefs which define his/her identity and delineate his/her preferences over behaviour at that time and in that context (Finnemore & Sikkink 1998: 904; Risse, Ropp & Sikkink 1999, 2013). Constructivist theorising commits therefore to the mutual constitution of actors, driven by ideational structures (Price & Reus-Smit 1998: 266; Wendt 1999). This mutual constitution through shared ideational structures limits constructivist explanatory insights into ASEAN's order. For constructivists, ideational structures are an expression of inter-subjective belief – i.e., a community of same meaning – and this shared sameness constrains/ shapes/constitutes agents (Florini 1996: 364). Inter-subjectivity exists as collective knowledge that is shared by all (Adler 1997: 327) and *cannot* be reduced to the beliefs of any given individual (Finnemore & Sikkink 2001: 393).

The message is clear – inter-subjectivity creates a uniformity of internalised beliefs; the same belief is internalised in the same way and has to mean the same thing to all parties who hold that belief. These beliefs are not static and can change through processes of socialisation and learning (Onuf 1989: 96–7, 111; Wendt 1999: 82, 101–2, 123). This framework powers the discussion of security communities in general, and their potential in ASEAN in particular. Claims that Southeast Asian order is predicated on a security community in turn rest upon the existence of peaceful norms that create morally preferable inter-subjective beliefs of practitioners towards peace and non-interference.

Work on rituals, however, makes no assumption about the necessity of shared meaning and in doing so opens up new explanatory opportunities. Rituals can foster common action without requiring common beliefs (Kertzer 1988: 11, 96) or, as Roger Keesing puts it, 'because meanings depend so heavily on what individuals know, the same ritual sequence ... may evoke highly diverse meanings' (Keesing 2012: 407).[9] This position has been echoed by those working on regulatory theory. Hilary Charlesworth and Emma Larking's analysis of 'human rights ritualism' with regard to the United Nations system focuses on how and why

---

[9] There is debate within the study of ritual about its relationship with meaning and experience. The closer the study is to disciplinary IR, the greater the assumption that ritual facilitates shared meaning. See Kratochwil (1989).

human rights are so widespread as a particular practice, but with very little shared sense of the importance of these values to individual states (Charlesworth & Larking 2014; Larking 2017; Charlesworth 2010). Charlesworth (2010: 12) defines ritualism in this context as a situation where 'there is no acceptance of particular normative goals, but great deference is paid to the formal institutions that support' those goals.

As such, a ritual and symbol approach emphasises the physical performance of regionalism and the documents, objects, art, and objectifications that are deployed during that performance. This focus on the practice, doing, and representation of politics shifts the locus of our explanatory accounts. Where constructivist accounts of order examine agreed texts and shared events for evidence of the creation of deeper shared meaning and a hidden inter-subjectivity, an account of order resting on ritual and symbol considers these texts and events as the things that generate order by creating shared experiences, even when those are interpreted in different ways.

1.4 Rituals and Symbols in ASEAN's Order

The reasoning outlined above provides the basis for the applied understanding of ASEAN developed over the rest of this work. The story of ASEAN's first thirty years, discussed in Section 2, is about a group of divided and weak states managing, in some way, to hang together. ASEAN's creation was a pit-stop in a period that began at the end of the Second World War and culminated in the mid-1970s. By 1976 the form of order that ASEAN promoted crystallised around maintaining co-existence, national freedoms, and opt-in regionalism. This was a form of 'ideal regionalism' – a vision of regional cooperation that all members could concur in the abstract was a good thing, but who also agreed that no substantive steps were necessary to achieve this vision. The outcome was the emergence of an accepted gap between the reality and rhetoric of the region. This gap was fraught with constant tension – too little regional activity and ASEAN would fall into obsolescence, too much activity and the unwillingness of states to actually agree would be exposed. This tension was managed by the development of ASEAN's habit of cooperation through an increasingly dense network of summits, meetings, and enduring conversations that, whilst not producing shared norms, developed a reflex to communicate. States would never let conversations trump their ability to act in their own self-interest, but neither would states allow acting in their self-interest signal the end of the conversation.

The combination of ideal regionalism versus immediate self-interest, and of rhetoric, reality, and enduring conversations, were the grounds upon which rituals and symbols grew. ASEAN elites created, sometimes accidentally and sometimes intentionally, a series of rituals and symbols that provided a sense of order to regional affairs. These rituals began in a very minimal way – for much of its early history, a key ritual moment occurred at the meetings of diplomats and politicians who were often in open disagreement with one another. The regular bringing together of these actors quickly developed into a shared set of expressions that were used to present regional politics.

Crucial in the Southeast Asian context was the role of the 'fathers of their country' – political leaders of great renown and long duration who occupied positions of significance in their respective country's history. Lee Kuan Yew, Singapore's prime minister (1959–1990, senior minister 1990–2004, and minister mentor until 2011), Mahathir Mohamad, Malaysia's prime minister (1981–2003 and 2018), and Suharto, Indonesia's president (1968–1998) are crucial figures. Whilst the political reputation of each varies, each occupied a leading position for an extended period of time and was able to attach their aura not only to ASEAN in general but to a vision of ASEAN in particular. Over time, heads of state and government became increasingly involved in ASEAN and provided a 'fixity' to its approach to regional affairs that has proven hard to shake. ASEAN elites presented themselves as bound by common traditions, invoking documents from the past to justify activities in the present, and imbuing them with symbolic importance. The end of the Cold War and ASEAN's membership expansion were crucial 'training experiences' for regional elites in terms of responding to challenges and crises in 'acceptable' ways and engaging with problematic issues without threatening ASEAN's core mission.

Section 3 explores ASEAN's more recent history, starting with the shock of the 1997 Asian financial crisis. The crisis was encountered by regional elites who had long histories of working within ASEAN and a continued commitment to the fundamentals of the regional project just described. The debate was never about how to transform ASEAN into something new; instead it was about how to save the ASEAN that already existed. At a time of intense competition about the needs, nature, and direction of ASEAN, emerging especially from non-elite and extra-regional sources, ASEAN ultimately decided to continue its traditional approach to regional affairs. The number of issues that ASEAN engaged in expanded considerably, and its institutional density increased, but the gap between rhetoric and reality did not close – indeed it widened as ASEAN made commitments in areas such as human rights and democracy which were far removed from the domestic realities of states. These reforms came about as responses to the crisis and to pressure from civil society and dialogue partners, and because of a fair degree of path dependency. ASEAN shifted from presenting an ideal regionalism to which all could agree, to a phantom regionalism where commitments to human rights and democracy, amongst others, did not even enjoy 'idealised' support. Phantom regionalism not only possessed the quality of the 'not yet real'; it had within it strong overtones of the unreal – something not only incongruous with the extant situation but shockingly unimaginable. This phantom regionalism was undergirded by a dizzying set of agreements, declarations, vision statements, and work plans produced in greater quantity, as if the unrealism of the project required greater 'pinning down' in words if not deeds.

As ASEAN developed in this way, rituals and symbols came to the fore to hold the regional grouping together and provided the foundation and justification for ASEAN's expansion into new and contentious issue-areas of governance. ASEAN developed a particular physical performance of regionalism that created sophisticated ceremonies, as seen in the *Guide*. The meetings of ASEAN officials are choreographed performances in which elites participate, represent to others, and experience for themselves the unity of the region. A crucial additional dimension of this performance of regionalism emerges in the written record, which reveals how ASEAN elites sought to present themselves. Here again we see repetition with the same phrases emerging. We also see the growing importance of 'historical invocation'. Key documents of ASEAN, such as the Declaration of the Zone of Peace, Freedom and Neutrality (ZOPFAN), the Bangkok Declaration, and TAC over time became symbols of what it means to be ASEAN and are now invoked repeatedly as subsequent generations grapple with reforming ASEAN. These are the 'sacred texts' of ASEAN regionalism which convey symbolic importance and are markers of legitimacy and continuity. It is no accident that the Bali Accords of 1976 remain widely invoked and quoted in contexts beyond the intentions of their original framers – key symbols of ASEAN regionalism played a central role in permitting and shaping the ongoing processes of reform as they became ways to traditionalise apparently radical ideas into the regional body. Rituals were also expanded to strengthen the presentation of unity in its substantive absence.

This work concludes in Section 4 which serves as both a conclusion for the discussion and an opportunity to look forwards, identifying potential risks that emerge from the intersection of ASEAN's approach to regional cooperation and ongoing power shifts in the Asia Pacific region. This final discussion emphasises that cooperation through ASEAN is not an automatic or unchangeable decision and that regional cooperation has always been, and shall continue to be, a choice for member states.

Adopting a rituals and symbols framework to understand ASEAN provides new perspectives on old debates. It explains the juxtaposition of ever more sophisticated regional commitments on paper with enduring violation of those commitments in practice. Rituals and symbols were not *creating* shared values; they gave the impression of shared values, which has created ASEAN's peculiar order – members can cooperate when they want and disagree, even interfere, when they wish. Rituals and symbols themselves were and are the things that constitute regional order, they were not representative of deeper values and identities which explained Southeast Asian politics. Regional elites assemble very frequently and perform unity with each other and to the wider public. Through their performance and the invocation of ritual and symbol, these states and their leaders pay great deference to ASEAN, whilst at the same time the values it is committed to realising are, in practice, sidelined over and over. Deference is paid to the symbols of the region and everyone stands as ASEAN's anthem is played. With the ceremonies complete, elites go back to arguing, disagreeing, and ignoring regional commitments.

ASEAN has helped avoid the most negative consequences of power politics in the region, and thus has escaped open and widespread military conflict, but not because of the institutionalisation of widely and deeply shared normative allegiance to values in the way that constructivists suggest. Instead, ASEAN has been successful because through it, states in the region have created a shared ritual and symbolic framework that allowed these goals to remain central, agreed, and safeguarded even when members' behaviour deviated from these goals. In this sense, ASEAN is a reassurance mechanism that limits spill-over. It does not matter that non-intervention is not deeply held across the region. What matters is that ASEAN displays the impression that these norms *are* deeply held, and as such serves as a blanket that occludes violation. In the absence of shared and deeply held norms, and despite the power politics that otherwise would have torn ASEAN apart, rituals and symbols have become the glue that holds ASEAN together. ASEAN is successful, but not in the way or for the reasons that the boosters would claim or, indeed, that sceptics would dismiss. This approach is, therefore, successful if viewed from the perspective of maintaining ASEAN itself and a particular form of inter-state peace. From a rival perspective, for example, from eliminating threats to regional peace, it is less successful. Indeed, the paradox of ASEAN is that in its creation of various ways to cover up activities that go against its stated principles, it plays a very real role in permitting those same activities to occur.

2 Inventing ASEAN: 1945–1997

This section has three aims – first, to present the absence of substantive common norms in the ASEAN project; second, to outline the endurance and activities of ASEAN despite this absence; and third, to argue that a central reason for ASEAN's staying power through this period was the emergence of a ritual approach to regionalism, seen in both the written record of ASEAN and its schedule of meetings and summits. I investigate these claims by charting the context in which ASEAN emerged, and its activities until the 1997 Asian financial crisis.

The founding of ASEAN via the Bangkok Declaration on 8 August 1967 is not the first entry in the history of Southeast Asian regionalism. The period from the end of the Second World War to 1976 can be thought of as a process of establishing the meaning and institutional form of Southeast Asia. As such, 1967 was just one stop along the road towards regionalism. This does not mean that by 1976 everything was finalised; rather, a decade after Bangkok, the key principles of ASEAN's approach to regionalism had emerged. What were these principles? First amongst them was that the region was a space for the performance of unity absent the need for any strong unifiers. ASEAN members *were* unified around the desire to ensure the enjoyment of their sovereignty and freedom, but unsurprisingly this proved barren soil in which to grow anything other than the weakest of regional structures. This was not an easy lesson to learn – efforts before the existence of ASEAN to institutionalise Southeast Asia had failed, and ASEAN's activities, such as trying to realise its Zone of Peace, Freedom and Neutrality (ZOPFAN), fell afoul of national self-interest in its first decade. This failure, however, was not as problematic as might have been expected – of importance was that ASEAN committed to a shared ideal vision, not that it took steps towards realising that vision.

The development of a shared ideal vision for regionalism was apparent in the 1976 Bali Accords, which are, again, best thought of not as representing shared substantive values, or even, given subsequent events, as much of a step towards the creation of those values. Instead, they served as a statement about idealised regionalism that all could unite around without agreeing on substantive, and painful, steps to achieve it. This idealised regionalism opened the door for rituals and symbols to play the role that they do today, as it created the necessity to find something to hold the region together in the absence of real progress towards these apparently shared commitments.

From 1976 to the early 1990s, this approach to regional affairs continued. Members slowly expanded ASEAN's institutional reach and sophistication without letting its failings imperil their commitment to it. At ASEAN's heart throughout this period was a fundamental tension. Member-states agreed to the viability and desirability of certain things but would deviate from them when they deemed it in their interest to do so. These deviations were accepted by other members and did not undermine the region. ASEAN was held together in this period by the increasingly prominent symbolic and ritualised life that served to generate a sense of membership and togetherness in the absence of any deeply held norms and despite the power politics that constantly pulled at regional ties. This approach to regionalism was not the result of conscious decision-making by political elites; rather, it resulted from a failure to develop a more substantive regional body alongside a continued decision that the region was a suitable vehicle for the realisation of national goals. The growing number of meetings and consultations that characterised ASEAN in this period helped develop the habit of regionalism.

This approach was reinforced in the 1990s by two related processes – the end of the Cold War, and the commencement of ASEAN's membership expansion to include more states in mainland Southeast Asia. The political and security challenges to ASEAN that the demise of global communism created were countered by an intensification of the performance of Southeast Asian region-alism – an increasing tempo of heads of state meetings, and a renewed focus on key documents in ASEAN's past as a way to frame the future. ASEAN's membership expansion was part of this response – both a way to expand the performance of regionalism and to exemplify the success and value of ASEAN as a regional body. Thus, on the eve of the 1997 Asian financial crisis, ASEAN had fulfilled the vision of its founders, but not in a way they would have expected. No major regional conflicts had emerged, and cooperation in areas such as economics had developed, albeit slowly and fitfully. ASEAN had defended sovereignty, non-intervention, and non-interference not by eliminat-ing all threats to them, but by limiting the extent to which violations of them imperilled the regional peace.

2.1 Establishing Regionalism: Southeast Asia from Decolonisation to the Bali I Accords

The term Southeast Asia was well-used by the time the foreign ministers of ASEAN's founding members met in Bangkok in 1967. It had originated in the Second World War to delineate the British-led Southeast Asia Command from other, American-led, theatres of war. What we now term Southeast Asia had no unified history prior to the experience of Japanese imperialism. Historically, multiple centres of civilisation and political order jostled for primacy in a region where geography, culture, religion, and economics blunted the quest for unity (for a historical overview, see Cribb 2018). Yet this absence of a unified history was not so much an impediment to regionalism as an opportunity for a particular approach to regional governance. The very artificiality of the term 'Southeast Asia' meant that it was a blank slate. It was, then, an organising principle that leaders could fill with their own meaning. The period from the mid-1950s to the 1976 Bali Accords represents a struggle to answer the questions: what was Southeast Asia, what was it for, and how would those goals be achieved?

2.1.1 Foundations: Why, What, How

Unsurprisingly, the key goal for the states of Southeast Asia in the 1950s was security. Security had a series of meanings to it. Most obviously it meant security from external interference – whether that was from other states in the region interested in pressing territorial claims, from colonial powers jealously guarding their remaining holdings in the region, or from superpowers and indeed communism.[10] Communism was more than just an external threat. The threat of internal insurgency, often communist in nature, was real, and speaks to the complexity of the region's geopolitics. States were keen, as just noted, to ensure independence from Western powers, but they were also keen to ensure Western powers remained involved when they worked alongside national governments to suppress communism. Another meaning of security involves the security of political elites atop the ruling apparatus of the state; elites shared a concern to secure their position by promoting economic growth and social stability.

The question was how, if at all, would these goals be meshed into some sort of international agreement? The 1950s saw two broad options. In pursuit of security, Southeast Asian states could choose between alignment or some sort of self-reliance (see Roberts 2012: section 1). The alignment option involved embedding Western powers directly into regional security. Here the great powers would be formally acknowledged as guarantors of the last resort, and regional states would as a result acknowledge their own inability to provide for their own security. The South-East Asia Collective Defence Treaty of 1954 led to the Southeast Asia Treaty Organization (SEATO), an effort to orchestrate

---

[10] Decolonisation by Western powers in Southeast Asia was an extended process. The United Kingdom (UK) formally left Malaya in 1957, and North Borneo, Sarawak, and Singapore in 1963, all of which formed Malaysia (from which Singapore soon departed). Brunei was not independent from the UK until 1984. Vietnam was never fully restored to French colonial rule after the Second World War, finally winning its independence after the Geneva Accords in 1954, by which time Paris had granted independence to Cambodia and Laos in 1953. Indonesia resisted the return of the Dutch after the Second World War and its independence was recognised in 1949. Finally, the US granted the Philippines independence in 1946.

regional security into a clear, pro-Western/anti-communist, direction. The only members from Southeast Asia were Thailand and the Philippines, who were joined by Australia, France, New Zealand, Pakistan, the UK, and the US. However, SEATO was soon moribund – too obviously a vehicle for US strategic interests to attract other states in Southeast Asia, an impression exacerbated as France struggled against independence movements in mainland Southeast Asia. The formal embedding of Western powers into regional security arrangements was at loggerheads not only with the desire for independence from these same states, but was also too overt a statement of political alignment for many.

The second path was self-reliance. This path was riskier inasmuch as it placed the burden on weak states, but it was more attuned to the sensibilities of the time and the ongoing process of decolonisation. It was not immediately clear, however, that Southeast Asia was the appropriate 'geographic container' in which states should cooperate. Self-reliance was central to the 1955 Bandung Conference of African and Asian states. From Southeast Asia, Burma, Indonesia, the Philippines, Thailand, and Vietnam (representatives of both North Vietnam and the then State of Vietnam were present) attended. Bandung resulted in a set of principles concerning independence and security in a decolonised world. It is worth enumerating the Bandung principles in full as they serve so clearly, as we shall see, as an inspiration for ASEAN's approach to regionalism:

1. Respect for fundamental human rights and for the purposes and principles of the Charter of the United Nations.
2. Respect for the sovereignty and territorial integrity of all nations.
3. Recognition of the equality of all races and of the equality of all nations large and small.
4. Abstention from intervention or interference in the internal affairs of another country.
5. Respect for the right of each nation to defend itself singly or collectively, in conformity with the Charter of the United Nations.
6. (a) Abstention from the use of arrangements of collective defence to serve the particular interests of any of the big powers.
   (b) Abstention by any country from exerting pressures on other countries.
7. Refraining from acts or threats of aggression or the use of force against the territorial integrity or political independence of any country.
8. Settlement of all international disputes by peaceful means, such as negotiation, conciliation, arbitration or judicial settlement as well as other

peaceful means of the parties' own choice, in conformity with the Charter of the United Nations.

9. Promotion of mutual interests and co-operation.
10. Respect for justice and international obligations (Bandung Conference 1955: 169).

Bandung illustrates the extent to which 1967 was embedded in an ongoing discussion about how the 'global south' arranged their affairs. Bandung articulated a code of conduct, revealed a reluctance to overtly align with either side of the Cold War, and showed a concern with flexibility and consensus (see Acharya & Tan 2008: 3–11). State security was to be achieved through an acceptance of an equal right to exist, combined with respect for domestic freedom, and a commitment to organisations such as the United Nations as a vehicle for state equality. Interestingly Bandung gestured towards some form of pan-regional cooperation across Asia and Africa, unsurprising given how decolonisation was affecting both regions. There was not an automatic assumption that 'Southeast Asia' was the appropriate vehicle for cooperation.

However, Bandung ultimately did not mark a decisive step towards pan-regional cooperation, and the African-Asian unity that it gestured towards did not materialise. The ideas that Bandung represented remained significant when, less than a decade later, Southeast Asian states sought to organise their affairs, this time on a more geographically limited basis. The first wholly indigenous step towards creating a Southeast Asian body came in 1961 when the Federation of Malaya (then consisting of peninsular Malaysia with Sarawak, North Borneo, and Singapore joining the federation on 16 September 1963), the Philippines, and Thailand met in Bangkok at the end of July to form the Association of Southeast Asia (ASA). ASA's founding documents spoke of various, ill-defined, cultural and economic cooperation, but its geostrategic alignment was never clear. Its members were broadly pro-Western, or at least strongly anti-communist, but were unwilling to position ASA clearly on the 'Western side' given parallel interests in non-alignment and national independence (Pollard 1970). ASA was undermined by the formation of Malaysia in 1963 which prompted the Philippines to renew its claims to North Borneo, fatally undermining cooperation between two ASA members at a vital time. The year 1963 also saw the short-life of Maphilindo, a regional association between the Federation of Malaya, Indonesia, and the Philippines agreed in Manila on 11 June 1963. Here discussion focused on the proposed creation of Malaysia and the Philippines' continued claim to North Borneo, and it was again this issue that led to Maphilindo's near immediate redundancy.

Three important points stand out in these precursors to ASEAN. First, states within the geographic region of Southeast Asia understood that there were possibilities at the regional level within the container represented by the label Southeast Asia to 'do something' – that the region was a suitable vehicle for national interest to be achieved. This 'do something' came from a resolve, expressed poetically but illustratively by Thai Minister of Foreign Affairs Thanat Khoman in reference to ASA that '[there was] a surge in our hearts to be masters in our own house and our abiding faith in the Asian culture and traditions and particularly in our capability to shape and to direct for ourselves the future destiny of our nations' (reported in Ness 1962). Second, the geopolitical preferences of individual states did not need to be formally mirrored in a regional commitment. Whilst individual states had preferences towards the United States, there were variations in how explicit that relationship could or should be. States remained strongly anti-communist in orientation and so to some degree 'in the Western camp' but, at the same time, did not necessarily want to make that position explicit or to lapse into a state of overt dependence on extra-regional states. Regional commitments could, therefore, be vague on this point and not retard the regional project more generally. Third, regional cooperation was not the outcome of resolving tensions even over the most fundamental of issues between members – it could be the mechanism through which those tensions were to be managed.[11] In other words, regionalism did not need to wait for the settling of border disputes and overlapping sovereignty claims; it could emerge amidst those tensions.

ASEAN's foundation was less of a turning point than it was part of a continuing process of crystallisation about both the size and geometry of regionalism and what it might achieve. Alice Ba (2009: section 2) argues that the foundation of ASEAN came at the confluence of shifting regional politics (the fall of Sukarno in Indonesia, Singapore's departure from Malaysia), increased worries over declining Western involvement in regional security (US difficulties in Vietnam and the British wind-down in Asia, both imperilling the anti-communist position) and the threat this posed to anti-communist elites, and a continuation of the belief that action at the regional level was representative of the self-determination of regional states. The 1967 Bangkok Declaration continued many of the themes present in Bandung and the previous abortive regional projects. As such the declaration was broad, calling for an acceleration of economic growth, social progress, and cultural development (article 2.1), promotion of regional peace and security through adherence to the principles of

---

[11] Illustratively, the Manila Accord at the heart of Maphilindo spoke not of resolutions but agreements to continue to discuss tensions in a civil manner. See United Nations (1963).

the United Nations (UN) Charter (article 2.2), and a range of technical cooperation. The most innovative commitments were institutional – the creation of regular meetings of foreign ministers (article 3a), a standing committee (3b), ad hoc committees and permanent committees as were thought necessary (3 c), and national secretariats (3d). The Bangkok Declaration was vague about the geopolitical leanings of the new organisation, noting only that members 'share a primary responsibility' for the safety of the region. Military bases run by external powers were 'temporary and remain only with the expressed concurrence of the countries concerned' (ASEAN 1967). Finally, it is worth remembering that ASEAN had a broader membership than either previous version of Southeast Asian regionalism; for the first time Indonesia, Malaysia, the Philippines, Singapore, and Thailand were together in a single regional framework.

The creation of ASEAN marked the moment when Southeast Asia was decisively chosen as the appropriate form of regionalism, and the commitments in the Bangkok Declaration reveal that this regional project was going to be broad rather than narrow. However, the declaration itself, little more than two pages long, provided no detail on how these commitments were to be realised. The process of constructing Southeast Asian regionalism continued for at least another decade as member-states jostled around competing visions of regionalism within the context that Bangkok had established. This near-decade of trial and error was characterised by two things – the failure to craft common positions on anything other than aspiration, and the continued investment of time and effort into the regional project despite this failure. As a result, ASEAN became something uniquely suited to the fractious region it represented, a mechanism through which regional and state stability and resilience could be achieved through the coexistence of different interests in a single accommodating framework.

First on ASEAN's agenda, true to the priorities of its members, was trying to establish the practical meaning of regional peace and security. To this end, in 1968, Malaysia proposed the neutralisation of Southeast Asia, suggesting that the region seek legal guarantees from external great powers to avoid competition in the region (Haacke 2005: 52–5). The Malaysian proposal was an attempt to terminate Southeast Asian states' security, defence, and alliance relationships with external powers and to cement the region as both formally neutral and explicitly self-reliant (Ba 2009: 73; Acharya 2001: 53).[12] As such it can be seen as a break with

---

[12] Malaysia's Foreign Minister Tun Razak, who proposed the idea, was thinking of an inclusive region including all states, not just the then five members of ASEAN.

precedent, which had blended together the desire for self-reliance with a varying degree of actual reliance on Western states. Malaysia's proposal, however, met with strong pushback. It was rejected by other ASEAN members as too sweeping a statement (Haacke 2005: 55–9), especially given that the Bangkok Declaration only the year before was less specific. ASEAN almost fell apart immediately after the Malaysian proposal as the Philippines and Malaysia faced off over competing claims to Sabah, nearly coming to blows and largely suspending ASEAN activity. That setback resolved peacefully, and member-states ultimately released, in 1971, the ZOPFAN declaration. ZOPFAN, in its substantive clauses, is incredibly short. It resolves that first, ASEAN members are determined to work towards the recognition and respect of Southeast Asia as a zone of peace, freedom, and neutrality (with no definition of the term or a timescale), and second that states in the region (note not ASEAN) should cooperate more (ASEAN 1971b).

The process of getting to ZOPFAN reveals something about ASEAN that remains true until today and was crucial in establishing how ASEAN would work. ZOPFAN was not a stepping stone to any substantive shared standards (as we shall see, ZOPFAN has never been realised), but this does not mean that it was wholly pointless. If it were irrelevant then regional elites were fools to create it and fools to keep mentioning it. ZOPFAN's significance arises from the fact that it was agreed and that states continued over the decades ahead to agree to it. ZOPFAN outlined an 'ideal regionalism' that all states could commit to in the abstract without making sacrifices to achieve it. Rhetorical commitments to 'ideal forms' could be made in the absence of much interest in working to substantively realise them. They were both binding points of agreement and ways in which disagreements could be accepted. In negotiating ZOPFAN, disagreements about the nature of the regional project did not result in a rejection of it. Malaysia stepped back from its initial proposal for full neutralisation and other countries did not read Malaysia's neutralisation proposal as a take it or leave it proposition. Instead ZOPFAN represents a continued vesting of importance in 'Southeast Asia' as an opportunity for regional states to discuss issues with each other. As such, ZOPFAN's true significance is found less in its role in creating regional norms and more in the fact that states, through ZOPFAN, performed their membership of ASEAN. ZOPFAN took on more symbolic importance, outstripping its direct real-world affect, and ASEAN elites repeatedly committed to realising ZOPFAN despite ongoing evidence that their actions did not live up to this commitment. This step towards idealised commitments and minimal implementation created the space for rituals and symbols to emerge and hinted at the emerging nature of ASEAN's order.

From 1971 until the Bali Accords of 1976, low-level but important activity occurred within ASEAN. Senior officials continued to refine what ZOPFAN meant, a 'search for consensus on basic principles' (Ba 2009: 77).[13] Work also continued in a range of functional activities. By 1976 ASEAN had developed, in line with the Bangkok Declaration, a range of permanent and ad hoc committees.[14] In this period, ASEAN followed an economics-first approach, not in negligence of the political goals it had set itself at Bangkok and in ZOPFAN, but because of them – 'economic co-operation not only paved the way for co-operation in other areas but was indeed an essential precondition for the achievement of [other] objectives' (Irvine 1982: 13). Three areas were to be showcased – the creation of preferential trading agreements, co-investments in coordinated industrial projects, and a policy of increasing industrial complementarity between ASEAN members (see Castro 1982: 80). Setting what became a reoccurring theme for ASEAN, progress in these fields was very slow. Illustrating the enduring security concerns and mistrust between ASEAN members, there were no meetings of economics ministers until 1975, everything before then being run through the foreign ministerial meetings (Colbert 1986: 196).

Additional insight can be generated by considering how ASEAN chose to represent itself even in this earliest of periods through examining the language that was used in the joint communiqués of the Annual Ministerial Meetings (AMMs). The second AMM, in August 1968, concluded that the meeting was 'held in an atmosphere of perfect cordiality, mutual understanding and goodwill' (ASEAN 1968: paragraph 10). Such language was impossible in 1969. The third AMM did not occur until December 1969 because of tensions over Sabah previously mentioned. Instead of an atmosphere of perfect cordiality, then, the third AMM recorded that Malaysian Prime Minister Tunku Abdul Rahman and Philippines Foreign Minister Carlos P. Romulo would restore diplomatic relations 'in the spirit of goodwill and friendship and because of the

---

[13] Ba offers a broadly positive narrative of the immediate fate of ZOPFAN after 1971, which can be contrasted with Acharya's (2001: 53–5) more sceptical reading of its short-term effect.

[14] There were permanent committees on food and agriculture, civil transportation, communications/air traffic services/meteorology, shipping, commerce and industry, media, finance, tourism, land transport and communication, science and technology, and socio-cultural activities. Thematic ad hoc committees had been formed on central banks and monetary authorities, synthetic rubber, sugar, and trade. Ad hoc committees also provided bureaucratic coordination in four areas – a special coordinating committee for ASEAN, the Brussels Committee, a Geneva Committee and a committee on the idea of an ASEAN secretariat. An additional ad hoc committee met to discuss coordination of support for Indochina states in the wake of the Vietnam War.

great value Malaysia and the Philippines placed on ASEAN' (ASEAN 1969: paragraph 2). Again, ASEAN was being framed as the vehicle that resolved regional discord.

Cordiality was restored, at least linguistically, at the fourth AMM held in Manila in March 1971 which noted that the '[m]eeting was concluded in the traditional spirit of ASEAN cordiality and mutual understanding' (ASEAN 1971a: paragraph 13). In every AMM between 1971 and 1976, the same articulation was used, and 'the traditional ASEAN cordiality' was invoked at the end of each document. What does ASEAN cordiality refer to? The Bandung principles, listed earlier, provide part of the answer in terms of goals, but to this we should add the procedural practices of ASEAN, notably the famous commitment to consultation, consensus, discreetness, informality, pragmatism, expediency, and non-confrontation that were being developed and experienced as regional elites engaged with each other through ASEAN (Acharya 1997: 328–9). It is interesting to see how these practices became central to the representation of ASEAN regardless of their nature or the degree to which they were followed. Part of this is the very quick invocation of tradition to describe this approach; after only four years, the AMM was referring to 'traditional' ASEAN, which whilst premature in any plausible meaning of the word 'traditional', represents an attempt to give the practices that were already emerging in Southeast Asian regionalism greater status. 'Traditional' is an invocation of a particular interpretation of the past that, whilst not wholly untrue, was certainly not completely accurate.

2.1.2 The 1976 Bali Accords

Although prime ministers and presidents had attended the AMMs if they were held in their country, the meetings of the first nine years of ASEAN were conducted at ministerial level and below. This separation of the highest levels of political authority from ASEAN ensured that any failure of the regional project remained disassociated from the personal prestige of national leaders. By 1976 the situation had changed, especially with the final defeat of South Vietnam in the previous year and continued uncertainty in Indochina. In this context, the first ASEAN Heads of Government meeting in Bali, held in the 'traditional ASEAN spirit of friendship and cordiality', reviewed ASEAN since 1967, cemented the ASEAN approach to regional affairs, and set the parameters for ASEAN's forthcoming activities (ASEAN 1976b). Most importantly it saw the agreement of two key documents, the Treaty of Amity and Cooperation (TAC) and the Declaration of ASEAN Concord. The Bali Accords should be seen as the full flowering of ASEAN's 'idealised regionalism' vision and the key moment when the quest for uniform positions shared between ASEAN members was replaced with verbal commitments to a regional unity.

TAC explicitly invoked Bandung (1955), the Bangkok Declaration (1967), and ZOPFAN (1971) in order to 'promote regional peace and stability through abiding respect for justice and the rule of law' (ASEAN 1976c: preamble). This linkage helped present a region both of consistent ideas and linear development. Most famously, ASEAN members agreed that their mutual relations would be guided by six principles:

a. Mutual respect for the independence, sovereignty, equality, territorial integrity and national identity of all nations;
b. The right of every state to lead its national existence free from external interference, subversion or coercion;
c. Non-interference in the internal affairs of one another;
d. Settlement of differences or disputes by peaceful means;
e. Renunciation of the threat or use of force;
f. Effective cooperation among themselves (ASEAN 1976c: article 2).

Beyond that, TAC is full of vague commitments to cooperate more fully in areas across economic, social, technical, scientific, and administrative fields. As had now become usual for ASEAN, the specificity that would be required for these commitments to be realised was absent from the document. TAC was a treaty rather than a declaration, and was framed as legally binding. It even contained a dispute resolution system, the High Council, which would serve as a mediating body and, where invited, offer appropriate measures for the 'prevention of a deterioration of the dispute' (ASEAN 1976c: article 15).

The Declaration of ASEAN Concord contained some of the detail that was lacking in TAC. The declaration adopted what would become ASEAN's standard tripartite division between political, economic, and social cooperation, and in doing so offers a useful insight into the meaning of the regional project in 1976. Under political cooperation the ASEAN Summit process was institutionalised and regularised, albeit 'as and when necessary'; 'immediate consideration' was to be given to 'initial steps' towards realising ZOPFAN; and solidarity was to be strengthened through promoting the harmonising of views (ASEAN 1976a: A1). The economics cooperation field, always the most active of ASEAN, took up the most space with more detailed activities in the areas of food and energy, industry, and trade, building upon ASEAN's economics-first approach. Social cooperation focused on the well-being of low-income groups, rural population, women, and youth as well as concern about thematic issues such as population growth (ASEAN 1976a).

What are we to make of these documents? Treaties, by their very nature, are intended to be legally binding on those who ratify them, in contrast to declarations. Yet ASEAN member-states did not live up to TAC, and this 'shortcoming' was completely legitimate. The High Council was never activated, and states' behaviour continued to violate the standards of practice outlined.[15] Both TAC and the Declaration of ASEAN Concord have been microscopically examined for evidence that they created, represented, solidified, or in some other way augmented regional norms (Kahler 2000 analyses TAC in relation to its role in legalisation). However, given the failure to live up to these standards in reliable ways – as discussed later – another interpretation is preferable. Mirroring ZOPFAN, but now writ large across all areas of ASEAN activity, these two documents provided a vision of how regional affairs should be organised in a way that all ASEAN members could agree was desirable – that in a perfectly peaceful world, both domestically and internationally, members could agree that these standards would guide their behaviour in a reliable way. ASEAN unity was displayed and intensified, without it actually being realised. In this way, TAC and the Declaration of ASEAN Concord would come to represent the failure of regionalism to produce deeply shared values that shaped behaviour, and the success of regionalism in producing displays and documentation that remained important over time. As such, framing an agreement such as the *Treaty* of Amity and Cooperation was a signalling device, differentiated from a declaration or agreement, which conveyed the seriousness of regional decision-makers and marked their confidence of and value in ASEAN. It marked a new level of sophistication for regional cooperation, separate from how TAC would actually be used. This did not mean that ASEAN would achieve nothing in the realm of technocratic governance. Especially in the economics field, there was clear evidence of coordination which bore fruit in the future, albeit at a slow rate. Yet for ASEAN's core business – securing peace and security for the region – success was more the product of ignoring violations to this ideal order under the rhetorical cover of TAC, rather than abolishing them.

2.2 Stasis or Stability? ASEAN between 1976 and 1991

The period from 1976 to the 1990s offers valuable insights into ASEAN's emerging approach to regional governance. The most important issue that

---

[15] On the weakness of the High Council, see the discussion in Caballero-Anthony (1998: 49–50), drawing on Muntarbhorn (1986).

ASEAN faced throughout the 1980s was the ongoing situation in mainland Southeast Asia. After assuring ASEAN members in late 1978 that it would respect the principles of sovereignty and non-intervention, Vietnam invaded Cambodia (known as Kampuchea under the Khmer Rouge government). The invasion threatened regional security – the Soviet Union publicly backed Vietnam and China invaded Vietnam in 1979, albeit with little success. Vietnam also directly threatened Thailand, and there was a series of skirmishes between Thai and Vietnamese forces as the latter operated inside Cambodia. As such the situation in mainland Southeast Asia throughout much of the 1980s directly challenged ASEAN's desire to bring peace and security to the region and, through the direct involvement of external powers, tested Southeast Asia's nominal autonomy and its right to determine its own destiny.

ASEAN took a leading role in responding to the crisis. The Vietnamese had expected that overthrowing the Khmer Rouge regime would meet with international approval. Instead, outside of the Soviet Union and its allies, the reaction was one of broad condemnation. ASEAN led calls to isolate Vietnam and the Hanoi-backed government of Kampuchea. ASEAN further called for the withdrawal of Vietnam from Cambodia and for fresh elections to create a national government. ASEAN's position was not one of neutrality and non-intervention. Instead, it pursued a policy of confrontation with, and ultimate reversal of, Vietnam's actions. ASEAN's position, however, and its ability to pursue it reasonably coherently over the 1980s could not be attributed to a natural harmony of interest between ASEAN members. Thailand led the anti-Vietnamese position, but Bangkok's concern was just as much about the geopolitical consequences of a Vietnamese-dominated Indochina as it was a defence of principles of sovereignty and non-intervention, a concern shared by Singapore and Malaysia. Indonesia, by contrast, viewed China as the largest threat and was worried that a weakened Vietnam would be unable to act as a buffer between ASEAN and China (Alagappa 1993: 452–3). Indonesia was especially concerned lest ASEAN's pointed approach make the realisation of ZOPFAN more unlikely by further entrenching great power competition in the region (Leifer 1989: 155).

These diverging views illustrate the very real limits of ASEAN's cohesion with respect to the norms that are sometimes assumed to characterise that region. Calculations of self-interest were more prevalent than any strict adherence to non-intervention. Yet the coexistence of this divergence with ASEAN's action also illustrates that member-states were willing to work together even when their narrow national interests pulled in different directions. A byproduct of this decade of focus on a single pressing issue was, as Carlyle Thayer (1990: 157) remarked, the development of a 'close-knit pattern of consultation and coordination' amongst ASEAN members that might not otherwise have occurred. This consultation was a vital part of regionalism – the continued agreement to consult during and after disagreements was a crucial ingredient in habitualising regionalism. The juxtaposition of habit and norm violation can be seen in the Manila Summit of 1987, which made direct reference to the internal affairs of the Philippines, calling for a peaceful resolution of disputes between President Ferdinand Marcos and opposition leader Corazon Aquino. The joint statement of the five other ASEAN members was explicit: '[w]e call on all parties to restore national unity and solidarity so as to maintain national resilience' (Singapore Government 1986). This 'egregious example' (Haacke 1999: 583) of interference again illustrates the extent to which ASEAN's norms and written frameworks did not limit the activities of the states who had so solemnly written them into supposedly binding treaties. Such activities clearly showed the paradoxical nature of ASEAN's order – the defence of national freedom resulted in the protection of a state's freedom to interfere in the affairs of other members when it was deemed appropriate to do so. Through TAC especially, ASEAN allowed such activities as it ensured they were both controlled and ultimately received in a way that retarded their escalation into crisis.

Beyond politics, the period after 1976 was one of considerable economic growth in Southeast Asia, as countries moved towards export-led and market-oriented growth strategies. ASEAN's focus on regional economic coordination had been restated in Bali in 1976, and activities proceeded across trade, industry, finance, food/agriculture/forestry, minerals, transport, and tourism (Colbert 1986: 197). Various ASEAN committees, centres, and corporations were established building upon the earlier institutional forms developed, with the increasing engagement of economics ministers who now met directly to coordinate efforts. During the 1980s little, if any, progress was made in developing the complementarity of regional economics, and so they continued to be largely competitive in nature. ASEAN's economic achievements are thought of as 'modest' in general, and shortcomings 'particularly glaring' in the areas of industry and trade where most ink had been expended in prompting cooperation (Chatterjee 1990: 78). Whilst there was a move forward in the creation of preferential trade agreements (PTAs), the devil was in the detail.

The 'flexible conditions' of these PTAs meant that states were free to exclude products from them as they saw fit, enabling those goods excluded to be subject to import taxes. Thailand excluded some 63 per cent of its imported goods in this manner (White III 2000: 184). The result was that where free trade was agreed, it would often be in peripheral areas; one preferential trade agreement was reached to free up the trade of snowploughs in Southeast Asia, a rather unlikely market. Humorous as this may be, it illustrates the conundrum that

ASEAN faced – real integration required real and deep changes to national economies, something which states were not willing to do. The alternative was the emerging preference for pursuing integration where costs were low. In turn this suggested a very limited willingness to pay political costs, or use political capital, on ASEAN where resistance could be expected. The third ASEAN Summit, held in Manila in 1987, saw some relatively minor efforts to promote trade through expanding preferential trade agreements, but it represented 'more of the same' rather than any great steps forward. So tightly controlled was the summit that leaders were only on the ground for twenty-four hours and there were just sixty-five minutes dedicated to actual deliberation (Frost 1990: 23). It would be hard, however, to attribute national economic success to regional economic planning, and Srikanta Chatterjee (1990: 58) said it best of ASEAN's economic performance in this period when he noted that the strength of the region came 'more from the rapid growth and development performance of some of its [ASEAN's] member economies than the collective strength and cohesion of the association itself'.

2.3 ASEAN into the 1990s: The End of the Cold War and Expansion

The Cold War had, in two interrelated ways, supported the ASEAN that had developed since 1967. First, it had provided the broad geostrategic predictability in which ASEAN had been able to find a role. Regardless of ZOPFAN, there was a consistent alignment with the United States, unsurprising given the capitalist economies that were booming across the region. Second, in line with perceived Cold War imperatives, the US had downplayed the need for liberal democracy on 'its' side of the competition. Strong authoritarian states, if broadly capitalist in economic outlook, were either welcomed by the US in its struggle against communism or, at the least, not openly criticised. With the Cold War at an end, the US, its allies, and the emerging global civil society became much more strident in their promotion of liberal democracy and, as a result, more critical of capitalist authoritarians. The period immediately after the Cold War was thus a moment of increased uncertainty for Southeast Asia. ASEAN responded to this uncertainty through the invocation of history, mobilising the oft-violated TAC as a way to understand and control the future of the region.[16] Deeper than that, ASEAN survived, and thrived, because its

---

[16] In response to the push from Western countries, the early 1990s saw the emergence of the 'Asian values' debate, led by Southeast Asian states, which sought to blunt calls for universal civil and political rights in favour of a respect for cultural differences. The debate was widely criticised as a political attempt to deflect criticism from authoritarian and illiberal practices. See Bauer & Bell (1999); Bell (2000).

distinguishing between the emerging rituals of unity and the reality of it gave it great flexibility, as shown in its expansionist drive to 'complete' Southeast Asian regionalism. Both of these were crucial learning experiences for elites who would face the much greater challenge of the financial crisis in the late 1990s. Underpinning all of this was a fair degree of luck as economics across the region continued to thrive.

We see crucial evidence for how ASEAN was responding to the end of the Cold War in its schedule of meetings. Across both the regular AMMs and ASEAN Summits, held only in 1976, 1977, and 1987, but which now became increasingly regular, meeting three times between the end of the Cold War and the onset of the financial crisis (1992, 1995, and 1996 at an 'informal' summit), we see reference to TAC after a decade when it had not been mentioned at all. The 1992 Summit in Singapore noted that ASEAN would 'seek the cognizance of the United Nations for the Treaty [of Amity and Cooperation] through such means as an appropriate Resolution'. Whilst the heads of state claimed that this would 'signify ASEAN's commitment to the centrality of the UN role in the maintenance of international peace and security' (ASEAN 1992b: article 3), it also served as a process to recommit regional states to the symbolic importance of TAC to regional politics, especially coming off the 1980s where the document was largely ignored. This trend continued even more clearly at the AMMs. After 1976, the AMMs of ASEAN Foreign Ministers had not mentioned TAC in any of their joint communiqués. Yet from 1991, TAC was invoked in every AMM through to 1997. In 1991 TAC (and ZOPFAN) were referenced as 'appropriate bases for addressing the regional peace and security issues in the nineties' (ASEAN 1991: article 12). In 1992, alongside welcoming the accession of Vietnam and Laos to TAC, ASEAN Foreign Ministers invoked TAC as a guide for all parties to follow in the emerging issues in the South China Sea (ASEAN 1992a: article 17). The year 1993 saw the welcoming of the UN resolution on TAC, which was held to be 'significant in that it establishes a code of conduct and provides a mechanism for peaceful resolution of disputes' (ASEAN 1993: article 5). The following year again saw the reaffirmation of regional commitment to 'ASEAN's principles and objectives on regional peace and security' as articulated in ZOPFAN and TAC (ASEAN 1994). The significance of TAC was expanded through the desire to 'facilitate association with the Treaty but non-regional states' (ASEAN 1994). The following year, 1995, saw both Cambodia and Myanmar accede to TAC, and continued work on the best way to allow extra-regional states to accede to it (ASEAN 1995b: article 6), a conversation which was still ongoing in 1996 (ASEAN 1996).

ASEAN's summits also gave impetus to regionalism in Southeast Asia, although again the follow-through on commitments was weak. The 1992 Singapore Summit Declaration was split broadly into four – politics and security, economics, functional cooperation, and institutional matters. There was little sign of much substantive agreement, with ASEAN committing to 'seek to realise ZOPFAN' (now over thirty years after its original agreement and seemingly with no irony), and noting that it 'could use established fora' to promote dialogue (ASEAN 1992b). Economics was more developed, with a commitment to establish an ASEAN Free Trade Area (AFTA) by 2008 via a Common Effective Preferential Tariff. The importance of AFTA was emphasised in the institutional revisions to ASEAN, which saw the merger of various ASEAN economics committees into a single process, with a ministerial-level council being established to drive AFTA forward. In part to ensure ongoing leadership of ASEAN, leaders also agreed to now hold the ASEAN Summit every three years. Economics remained in the vanguard in 1995 in the Bangkok Summit Declaration, where finalisation of AFTA was brought forward to 2003 (ASEAN 1995a). We shall discuss the limits of economic integration in Section 3, but here it suffices to say that once again commitments to ideal regionalism continued apace, far outstripping the reality of the situation.

Another part of the strengthening of ASEAN's approach to regional affairs came from the realisation of the long-held goal of expansion. The mid-1990s witnessed Vietnam (1995), Laos and Myanmar (1997), and Cambodia (1999) join ASEAN. Expansion served many purposes for ASEAN; it turned previous enemies into close colleagues, expanded ASEAN's economic base, and hedged against Chinese expansion into the region. Expansion also served to demonstrate the 'Southeast Asia for Southeast Asians' pledge that had always been core to ASEAN's mission. The mechanism by which this expansion unfolded for each state was similar – an agreement on the part of the applicant state to accede to and respect all the treaties, declarations, and agreements of ASEAN. TAC held particular importance as it was acceded to before the date of application – Laos and Vietnam (1992), Cambodia and Myanmar (1995) – and was positioned as a prerequisite for ASEAN membership. The four states of mainland Southeast Asia had each experienced the workings of ASEAN prior to membership, enjoying observer status prior to membership being granted.

The behaviour of ASEAN's existing members and new members both before and after membership was granted suggests that their conduct rarely reached accordance with the principles to which they were agreeing. This was most egregiously the case in the mixture of attitudes and actions displayed relative to the question of Myanmar's membership in ASEAN. ASEAN followed a policy of 'constructive engagement' from 1991 in relation to Myanmar, itself an outgrowth of Thai policy towards their troublesome neighbour (Buszynski 1998). Two trends can be discerned, the first the attempt to get Myanmar to live up to TAC, especially important to Thailand given Myanmar's frequent military incursions across their mutual border. Here, non-intervention was something to be prioritised. The second trend, which cut across the first, was the interest on the part of some that constructive engagement be a way to change the behaviour of Myanmar's military junta, both because its domestic repression was so egregious and because this repression was pushing leading Western powers to pressure ASEAN to 'do something' about the issue. Whilst this did not reach the level of intervention that ASEAN engaged in with Myanmar in the 2000s (as discussed in Section 3), it clearly violated a strict interpretation of TAC. Lee Jones (2008: 274) quotes a source from Indonesia who said '"We are telling them very quietly, in a Southeast Asian way, without any fanfare, without any public statements: 'Look, you are in trouble, let us help you. But you have to change, you cannot continue like this'"'. This statement is worth unpacking because it illustrates the reality of a region quite at ease ('in a Southeast Asian way') with discussing domestic affairs whilst not letting that colour either broader relations or the ritualised presenta-tion of things like TAC as a behaviour-defining document.

2.4 ASEAN's Regional Mission

ASEAN's story is not limited to what it does within Southeast Asia. ASEAN has, since the 1970s, played a role in the wider relations of the Asia-Pacific and beyond. This took the form of a series of partnership agreements, the first being with Australia in 1974.[17] These agreements served to link ASEAN to the world around it, bring importance to the regional level as a node for activity, and augment the capacity of states in the region to engage with other powers as equals.

More central to ASEAN's ambitions in the wider world was institutional creation, most notably in this period the ASEAN Regional Forum (ARF) established at the 26th AMM held in Singapore in July 1993, and first meeting in 1994. The ARF was tasked with addressing the endemic security challenges facing states in the Asia-Pacific through a three-stage approach, intended to be gradual and evolutionary rather than simultaneous – confidence-building, developing preventive diplomacy, and developing conflict resolution mechan-isms (ASEAN Secretariat no date d). ASEAN was central to the workings of

---

[17] Today ASEAN has partnership agreements with Canada, China, the European Union, Germany, India, Japan, New Zealand, Norway, Pakistan, Russia, South Korea, Switzerland, and the US.

the ARF. The ASEAN Chair led the ARF and meetings occurred within ASEAN countries – most notably, the ARF meeting occurred immediately after the ASEAN summits. The first ARF meeting brought together ASEAN states (then six), its Dialogue Partners (Australia, Canada, the European Union, Japan, New Zealand, South Korea, and the US), its consultative partners (China and Russia), and its observers (Laos, Papua New Guinea, and Vietnam), creating a very wide membership. In one dimension the ARF, despite its gradualist approach, denotes ASEAN's ambitions at this time. In the post-Cold War, ASEAN was setting itself as central to the peace and security not only of Southeast Asia but the wider Asia-Pacific. TAC was specifically referenced in the Chairman's statement of the first ARF meeting as 'a unique diplomatic instrument for regional confidence-building, preventive diplomacy, and political and security cooperation' (ASEAN Secretariat 1994). The activities of the ARF before 1997 tacked closely to building confidence amongst participants through increasing dialogue on shared challenges, enhancing contact between defence staff, and increased information sharing (ASEAN Secretariat 1996).

Why did ASEAN create the ARF? Katsumata (2006) identifies three potential reasons – ASEAN sought to maintain US engagement with the region in the post-Cold War world, was seeking to enhance cooperation with China, and was driven to socialise its norms to the region. Katsumata prefers the third of these arguments, claiming that the norms of Southeast Asia were viewed as a preferable solution to broader Asia-Pacific problems. The focus on rituals and symbols allows for a fourth interpretation, one that offers new insights into the shortcomings of the ARF, and ASEAN's other external engagements, as we shall encounter in Section 3. As we have seen, ASEAN's approach to securing inter-state security had less to do with substantive norms shaping actor's social identity and more to do with performing a unity that was absent in reality. A crucial part of this was the knowingness of participants – that performing unity was something that allowed for acts of disunity. A similar interpretation can be applied to the ARF – that it was not intended to socialise those norms across such a diverse group of states, however desirable that might have been, but instead it was intended to expand the audience of ASEAN's rituals and, in so doing, enhance peace and security through increasing the performance of that peace and security.

2.5 ASEAN at Thirty

On the eve of the Asian financial crisis in 1997, ASEAN had developed into a successful regional organisation. For thirty years there had been no significant conflict in Southeast Asia. In the context of the regional situation in the early and mid-1960s, and with global competition through the prism of the Cold War, this was no small achievement. I have argued in this section that ASEAN achieved regional peace not through processes of embedding shared normative allegiances between members – the actions of these states make such claims implausible. Instead, ASEAN played a different role. ASEAN came to represent a stated 'ideal state' for regional affairs that, in turn, acted as a blanket under which violations of its principles could be bounded and so regional affairs inoculated against the contagion of insecurity. This ideal regionalism was not unknown to those working within ASEAN. Referring back to the pre-crisis ASEAN, ASEAN Secretary-General Rudolph C. Severino claimed that:

> There is no other way. In the real world, especially in the exceedingly diverse world of Southeast Asia, a balance has to be sought – and constantly adjusted – between what is desirable and what is possible, between the ideal and the practical, between ambition and reality, between desired ends and available means, between international involvement and national sovereignty (Severino 2000).

In the absence of thick shared values, the increasing number of meetings and consultations, the shared language to describe ASEAN, and the 'discovery' that ASEAN's history could be invoked to frame the present provide evidence of the emergence of a ritualised and symbolic form of regionalism that filled the gap between rhetoric and reality and, in so doing, held in check the centrifugal tendencies of power politics. This was the nature of ASEAN's order.

The end of the Cold War was not only a historical moment – it was a vital learning experience for how to respond to crisis. Rather than responding to external and internal challenges through the fundamental alteration of regional activity, intensification and expansion of agreed practice was the preferred approach. ASEAN overcame not by alteration but by intensification of the ritual and symbolic framework and the drawing in of heads of government to that web of display and representation. The crisis was an opportunity to demonstrate both the value of ASEAN and its ability to master challenges, both of which were ultimately achieved. The importance of the learning experience that the early 1990s represented is evidenced through examining the response of regional leaders to the much greater challenges posed by the 1997 financial crisis. This is the task of the following section.

3 Saving Regionalism: 1997–2017

This section describes and explains the significant changes to ASEAN in the two decades prior to 2017, sparked by the 1997 Asian financial crisis. Not only was the crisis a challenge to ASEAN, but with the benefit of hindsight, it also provided an opportunity for members to demonstrate that their approach, developed over the previous thirty years, had value. Their success in this was not easily won. ASEAN struggled to reconcile two competing pressures – the need to reform in light of the shortcomings of regionalism that the crisis had exposed, and the need to protect its particular contribution to regional affairs. The ultimate result was a process of community building that saw significant but partial reform. The range of ASEAN cooperation expanded significantly with deeper economic cooperation and revamped political-security cooperation sitting alongside engagement in new areas of concern, contentiously going so far as to include democracy and civil and political rights. As a result, ASEAN's institutional density rapidly increased, with more meetings, on more issues, and at more levels of government. Yet some things did not change. Most importantly the gap between commitments 'on paper' and reality remained wide, nurtured by a constant restatement of a traditional approach to non-interference. As such, compliance with regional commitments remained very low as states continued to prioritise their own interests.

To explain this process of community building and the changes/continuities that characterised it, I advance three claims. First, institutional redesign of ASEAN was slow off the mark as member-states jostled around different visions of regional governance – there was no grand plan for reform. Second, only when key symbols of ASEAN unity were invoked did these competing agendas align sufficiently to push forward regional reform. These symbols traditionalised and de-radicalised otherwise divisive issues in ASEAN and helped generate the consensus to proceed with institutional reform. The result of these inclusions, however, shifted ASEAN from an 'ideal region' where all members could agree that the 'on-paper' description was something they may all wish to see, to a 'phantom region'. Whilst the traditional idealism of inter-state peace and security remained, newer commitments were created with no sense that many members wished to see them fulfilled. Commitments to human rights, democracy, and good government may have been apparent on paper, but there was little evidence to suggest that these commitments were genuinely held by many ASEAN leaders. Third, as the challenges to ASEAN mounted as a result of its shift from ideal to phantom regionalism, so the display of unity through rituals became more important. More regular meetings offered the perfect opportunity to increase the formalism and public profile of ASEAN's ritual and symbolic environment. These actions and displays held the region together.

This section opens by framing the Asian financial crisis as a significant challenge to ASEAN as it exposed the limitations of its approach to regionalism. The immediate response was confusion, with competing challenges to ASEAN's aims and practices being made and rebuffed. The path forward emerged slowly and piecemeal, at the confluence of competing visions for regional reform and the invocation of ASEAN's past – most notably in regard to the Treaty of Amity and Cooperation (TAC) which grew in importance. The ASEAN Charter process locked ASEAN in a state of partial transformation. Balancing rival claims about ASEAN's future, the 2007 Charter solidified rather than overcame existing shortcomings. Crucial to the continued ability to address regional peace and security was the intensified ritual and symbolic life of ASEAN that had emerged in the first thirty years. ASEAN's failure to fully reform was thus the ultimate cause of its continued, if always limited, success.

3.1 Phantom Regionalism: Crisis, Contestation, and Symbols in Practice

The 1997 financial crisis started in Thailand with currency speculation against the baht in mid-May. The crisis had many causes, the most important being the structural weakness of poorly regulated capitalism in the region, the bursting of economic bubbles in key countries, and the resulting uncontrolled panic in financial markets (Radelet & Sachs 1998; Rüland 2000: 425). The previously booming economies of the 'Asian Tigers' ground to a halt amidst spiking unemployment, a collapse in trade, currency devaluation, and precipitous stock market declines. The inevitable consequence was social and economic distress on a larger scale than any other economic crisis in ASEAN's history, hitting the populations of members hard. These challenges, in turn, undid the smug complacency that had developed around ASEAN's regionalism. ASEAN and its leaders were framed as elitist, out of touch, and unable to deal with the challenges that the crisis had posed to the region.

Confusion, Contention and the Shift towards Phantom Regionalism: 1997–2004

The immediate response to the crisis saw open challenges by some political leaders to the traditional ASEAN approach to the procedural side of regional governance.[18] Malaysian Deputy Prime Minister Anwar Ibrahim, in July 1997,

---

[18] It is worth noting that the very presence of these challenges suggests that there were no shared norms around intervention/interference in any substantive sense prior to the crisis.

called for ASEAN to adopt a policy of 'constructive intervention', which he framed as a way for ASEAN members to more fully engage with each other to support the growth of civil society in order to promote stable and resilient societies. Although not itself a direct challenge to formal standards of non-intervention, the proposal opened the door to other, more radical, suggestions (Haacke 1999: 582). Thailand's Foreign Minister (and later ASEAN Secretary-General) Surin Pitsuwan openly advocated for what he termed 'flexible engagement'. Pitsuwan (1998) was clear that:

> ASEAN members perhaps no longer can afford to adopt a non-committal stance and avoid passing judgement on events in a member country, simply on the grounds of 'non-interference' . . . . if domestic events in one member's territory impact adversely on another member's internal affairs, not to mention regional peace and prosperity, much can be said in favour of ASEAN members playing a more proactive role.

Pitsuwan framed flexible engagement as working alongside, rather than replacing, ideas of non-intervention. This may seem nonsensical, but given our discussion of ASEAN, where on-paper commitments and state practices diverged in sustained ways, we can read flexible engagement as a proposal to formalise this state of affairs and so liberate discussion rather than radically overhaul ASEAN's approach to diplomacy. Pitsuwan's proposal was asking could not ASEAN do more if it was honest about how it really worked? ASEAN, however, had not worked on honesty so much as on a shared and accepted dishonesty, occluded from public acknowledgement by rituals and symbols. Pitsuwan's proposal was rejected in favour of ASEAN's existing approach of maintaining strict on-paper injunctions against interference and intervention which, as will be shown, continued to be violated.

The debate over flexible engagement was an important, but not the most important, consequence of the financial crisis. Of more significance was the regional response to the way that the crisis had caused such severe economic and social unrest. Between July and December 1997, the Thai stock market declined some 29 per cent, the Malaysian and Indonesian markets by almost 45 per cent, and the Filipino by 33 per cent (Goldstein 1998: 3). Regional currencies lost a large part of their value (Goldstein 1998: 2 notes that by May 1998 the Indonesian rupiah had lost 73.8 per cent of its value against the US dollar) and gross national product across the region declined, sometimes precipitously. Behind these macro-economic headlines, however, were the countless stories of how the individual lives of ASEAN's citizens were impacted by the crisis, and the suffering that resulted. ASEAN stood, through its apparent inability to address the crisis, as complicit in this suffering and as uncaring for the lives of those living within it.

ASEAN's response was to emphasise the caring dimension of much of its regional architecture. ASEAN Vision 2020, released in December 1997 as an initial response to the crisis, called on Southeast Asia to become 'a community of caring societies' (ASEAN 1997). The use of the word 'caring' only just predated the crisis; the Annual Ministerial Meetings (AMMs) and the ASEAN Summits had not used this word to describe ASEAN until the 1995 Bangkok Declaration where heads of state and government were 'desiring to create a caring, cohesive and technologically advanced ASEAN community' (ASEAN 1995a). The word 'caring' then filtered through to the 29th AMM in Jakarta, where foreign ministers 'emphasized the need to strengthen the family as a foundation for a strong caring and cohesive society' (ASEAN 1996: paragraph 38). Before this, even as ASEAN developed a range of cooperative endeavours that could be broadly grouped under the label 'social', it had never called for members to become caring. After the crisis, 'caring' made regular appearances in summit statements and AMM final communiqués.

Whilst the word 'caring' substantively means nothing, it was a useful immediate response to the anguish caused by the crisis. In Vision 2020, although it was placed next to terms such as 'total human development', and commitments to address hunger, malnutrition, deprivation, poverty, social justice, and the rule of law, no operational detail was provided (ASEAN 1997). This ambiguity is central to the story of regional reform. Words could be agreed upon because they were not particularly contentious. However, whilst ambiguity could promote agreement, it also opened the door to future specification as states struggled, often under pressure from civil society, to realise what that meant. This would have been problematic in ASEAN of the 1980s; it was made all the more difficult in 1997 because of the growing diversity of ASEAN's members.

Indonesia, ASEAN's *primus inter pares*, began a process of domestic trans-formation (Ahmad & Ghoshal 1999: 773). The financial crisis had exacerbated tensions in Indonesia as Suharto approached his thirtieth year in power, and Indonesia's mishandling of the consequences of the financial crisis further eroded his position (MacIntyre 2003). Suharto resigned on 21 May 1998 and was replaced first by B. J. Habibie, his vice-president, then Abdurrahman Wahid, and ultimately Megawati Sukarnoputri. This dramatic shift was significant for regional governance. Indonesia exercised significant 'behind-the-scenes' influence. A democratic Indonesia, and the emergence of a vibrant Indonesian civil society, would be an important driver for regional reform with its own ideas about what caring societies meant, tending unsurprisingly towards a complete embrace of democracy. Indonesia's move to democracy was balanced, however, by the consequences of the policy of expansion detailed in Section 2. ASEAN's expansion had been planned during the early 1990s, well before the financial crisis unfolded, as a triumphant moment – a vindication of the success and stability of ASEAN in the post-Cold War era. Now ASEAN had to develop commitments to caring societies in the context where CLMV (Cambodia, Laos, Myanmar, and Vietnam) countries, holding very different views, exercised the same rights of membership alongside a democratising Indonesia. All members not only with legitimate claims to the commitments to non-intervention and non-interference, but also with substantial procedural power within ASEAN and over its future, had to agree to the future reforms. Any pressure to move towards a stronger embrace of democracy, civil and political rights, or any other form of regional oversight was going to be scrutinised and strongly resisted by the new members who had, in part, joined ASEAN to ensure their domestic freedoms (Croissant 2004).

Vision 2020 did not offer a clear plan for the future of regionalism in Southeast Asia; nor should it be seen as the starting point of a linear and inevitable process culminating in the ASEAN Charter. Regional reform was not the product of a carefully crafted and executed masterplan in 1997. Rather, it was an organic accretion of ideas that drew on ASEAN's existing approach and the input of a small circle of trusted external sources, whilst reacting to external pressure and internal issues. The key issue that ASEAN's expanded membership faced was how to follow through on Vision 2020. The legitimacy of the regional grouping needed to be enhanced in the eyes of a very sceptical public. Existing regional priorities, especially peace and security, could not be undermined, and any reform needed to be agreeable to ASEAN's diverse membership.

Vision 2020 contained the seeds of how regional leaders would address this issue. Invocation of the past was crucial as a justification for the novelty that Vision 2020 contained. Heads of state and government re-affirmed their 'commitment to the aims and purposes of the Association as set forth in the Bangkok Declaration of 8 August 1967'. TAC was again rolled out and envisioned as 'functioning fully as a binding code of conduct for our governments and peoples' (ASEAN 1997). The Zone of Peace, Freedom and Neutrality (ZOPFAN) was also present, with 2020 declared as the year by which the 'full reality' of its commitments would be functioning. Although these commitments had not been fulfilled over the previous twenty years, their invocation of the past played a new role of traditionalising the new into the context of the old. By reiterating that documents like TAC retained an on-paper importance, ASEAN members were reassured that the areas of novelty in Vision 2020, especially around this slippery concept of caring communities, were tightly bounded.

This fusion of new and more traditional concerns was reflected in the Report of the Eminent Persons Group (EPG) on Vision 2020. The product of a series of meetings and discussions in 1999 and 2000, the EPG was charged with thinking through what the leaders' statement in Vision 2020 meant. The report advocated against ASEAN supranationalism, although it noted that the growing number of meetings and institutions that comprised ASEAN posed challenges to coordination (ASEAN 2000). The EPG suggested that ASEAN approach the question of reform with a view to promoting two themes – 'human security and development' and 'the people's ASEAN' (ASEAN 2000: 12). In this way, ASEAN would empower the peoples and civil societies of ASEAN members. For a long time, ASEAN had spoken of national and regional resilience as its aims. To this, the report suggested adding personal resilience which could be improved by individual rights and civil responsibilities, gender equality, religious tolerance and racial harmony, poverty reduction, employment and training, educational access, health and food security, and promotion of cultural diversity (ASEAN 2000: 12). The explicit mention of rights, even when twinned with the notion of responsibilities, was new, but the more general category of concerns was not. The 1995 Bangkok Summit Declaration, for example, under the banner of functional cooperation, spoke of ASEAN's artistic heritage, the need for social wellbeing, building educational capacity, social justice, eradicating illiteracy, participation of women in all fields of society, health cooperation, combatting drug addiction, and engaging civil society (ASEAN 1995a).

The report also called for a more coordinated approach to ASEAN governance, noting that the responsibility to drive ASEAN forward should sit with heads of government, not ministers (ASEAN 2000: 27). Underneath an intensified set of meetings of regional leaders, an expanded array of ASEAN institutions was imagined, cutting into previously unexplored areas in education, science, and governance (ASEAN 2000). The report further noted the need to develop a more coherent system of internal governance, not only amongst leaders, but by reaching out to other institutions such as universities. Underpinning this was a proposal for an expanded ASEAN Secretariat to support a new suite of functions – working more coherently with national administrations, ministers, and senior officers, and engaging with civil society and other intentional organisations. Whilst there is no evidence that this was planned at the time, the increasing regularity and number of ASEAN meetings, which built upon the habitual cooperation that had emerged since the 1980s, provided the necessary opportunity for the dramatic sophistication of ASEAN's ritual life, as discussed at the end of this section.

The period between 2000 and 2004 was a test of ASEAN's ability to mesh together new and old dimensions of regionalism in a system where very diverse members held an effective veto over the process. The Declaration of ASEAN Concord II (Bali II) served as a moment of solidification for ASEAN and its reform process. The opening paragraph invokes Bali I of 1976, tying the two documents together across the intervening twenty-seven years. New and old were artfully woven together. ASEAN members were 'conscious of the need to further consolidate and enhance the achievements of ASEAN as a dynamic, resilient and cohesive regional association' (ASEAN 2003: preamble). State commitment to the 1976 ASEAN Declaration (1976), ZOPFAN (1971), and TAC and the Declaration of ASEAN Concord (1976) was reaffirmed. To drive the point home as strongly as possible, the principle of non-interference and consensus in ASEAN cooperation was framed as of 'fundamental importance' (ASEAN 2003: preamble). Such a juxtaposition continued the momentum around the call for action whilst also framing that action as conservative. None of the most important of ASEAN's previous commitments were rejected or open for discussion. On paper, there was a seamless and single journey forward where every decision was the necessary prerequisite for the next decision.

The biggest innovation of Bali II was the formal commitment to creating a single ASEAN Community, comprising three pillars of activity – political/ security, economic, and socio-cultural. These pillars reflected existing areas of ASEAN activity, but formalised and institutionalised those actions into a more coherent whole. The ASEAN Security Community was dedicated to the peaceful processes of dispute settlement and a full recognition of sovereign rights (ASEAN 2003: A1, A2). The ASEAN Economic Community re-dedicated the organisation to the realisation of a single market and production base, aimed at stronger implementation of existing agreements such as the ASEAN Free Trade Area through the creation of new mechanisms (ASEAN 2003: B3). The ASEAN Socio-cultural Community 'envisaged' a region bonded together in partnership as a community of caring societies, realising commitments that dated back to 1976 and Bali I (ASEAN 2003: C1, C2).

The greatest example of how the new could be traditionalised came in the most contentious and problematic of issues for ASEAN – human rights and democracy. Bali II was quiet on the issue of human rights and democracy, using instead the vague language of caring societies. Yet the 2004 Vientiane Action Programme (VAP) marked, on paper, a radical development. Democracy was now a key theme of regional cooperation. ASEAN now aspired to 'achieve peace, stability, democracy and prosperity' (ASEAN 2004: 6). Human rights were now explicitly mentioned, and promoting them was a key part of realising the ASEAN Security Community. Human rights promotion was central, again on paper, to securing the inter-state peace and security that ASEAN held dear.

Yet all was not as it seemed. First the Annex to VAP which outlined suggested activities that could be undertaken to help realise commitments was more circumspect – for example, to achieve human rights, it advocated such activities as stock-taking, public awareness, and engagement in issues of migrant workers and women and children. There was no call for a radical reorientation towards any ASEAN-level oversight of human rights within member-states. Second, the origin of these commitments illustrates just how traditionally they were being understood. An elite-level civil society group, the ASEAN Working Group for the Establishment of a Human Rights Mechanism, had been advocating since the late 1990s for ASEAN to engage more fully with human rights concerns. Yet the Working Group did more than just advocate for human rights – it explicitly de-radicalised human rights by framing them as the solution to ASEAN's need to implement Vision 2020, and it even went so far in 2003 as to indicate that human rights were a mechanism for realising ASEAN's Security Community plans.[19]

The consequence of these changes was that by 2004, ASEAN had moved away from outlining an 'ideal regionalism' towards what I term 'phantom regionalism', at least in regard to its newer commitments. Previously, all states in ASEAN could agree that regional peace and security achieved through non-interference and a strong defence of sovereignty was desirable, even if they did not agree to limit their immediate freedom of action to achieve this goal. This remained the same. However, it was a very different case for ASEAN's newer commitments. As he departed the office of ASEAN Secretary-General in January 2013, Pitsuwan (2013) exhorted that 'we must build an ASEAN Community based on the values of freedom, democracy, human rights, human dignity and human security'. There is no evidence that many ASEAN members agreed with this statement. The repressive policies of so many ASEAN members suggest that this exhortation did not represent an idealised consensus. This does not mean that ASEAN regionalism was suddenly pointless or nothing more than a charade – it continued to function, as described in Section 2. Instead, the 'core ASEAN business' was now juxtaposed with areas of innovation where no agreement actually existed, even in the most idealised of forms.

---

[19] For a more complete review of the activities and importance of the Working Group, see Davies (2013b); Tan (2011).

Before moving on it is worth noting that the story of ASEAN from crisis to 2004 can be read as a vindication of the approach to regionalism that ASEAN developed prior to 1997. In the face of grave challenges, and despite the growing diversity of its members, ASEAN's constituents remained committed to diplomacy and cooperation – they continued to see ASEAN as a suitable vehicle for their time, attention, and resources. True to ASEAN's approach, this had not seen the harmonisation of member-state interests so much as a willingness to find ways to align competing demands into a single framework of cooperation. The price paid for this approach was that this cooperation was always more nominal than substantive, but the benefit was that ASEAN's fundamental goal of coexistence amidst diversity was protected. If the crisis was a challenge to ASEAN, the way it was overcome provided eloquent testimony to ASEAN's peculiar importance and an opportunity to perform ASEAN.

The ASEAN Charter Process: 2005–2007

The mechanics of drafting the ASEAN Charter, intended to wrap up the process of institutional reform sparked by the financial crisis and reset ASEAN on renewed foundations, was launched at the 11th ASEAN Summit in December 2005 and had two stages. An EPG of notables and dignitaries from across the region was set up to produce a series of recommendations. Members of the EPG served in personal and independent capacities, not as representatives of their governments (ASEAN 2005). It would be incorrect, however, to assume that these individuals were anything other than carefully chosen insiders – for example, the Indonesian representative was former Foreign Minister Ali Alatas. The EPG report was to be passed to a High-Level Task Force (HLTF) of active politicians for their consideration and drafting of a final text. This text would be passed to the heads of state and government for final agreement.

The EPG handed down its report in December 2006. The economic recommendations were comparatively modest, noting that fragmentation remained a key problem and that ASEAN should step up efforts to correct this. However, the discussion about the ASEAN Security Community was anything but pedestrian. The first principle that the report recommended was the 'promotion of ASEAN's peace and stability through the active strengthening of democratic values, good governance, rejection of unconstitutional and undemocratic changes of government, the rule of law including international humanitarian law, and respect for human rights and fundamental freedoms' (ASEAN 2006b: 2). The phrase 'active strengthening' was novel, inferring some sort of proactivity on the part of ASEAN in promoting a particular set of values. A similar disregard for non-interference was reflected in the suggested prioritisation of democracy as the most appropriate form of domestic governance. Absent from the fundamental principles and objectives that ASEAN outlined was any mention of ASEAN's traditional approach to regional affairs. Instead the report stated that 'the Charter should update ASEAN's principles and objectives in line with the new realities', perhaps the most aggressively revisionist statement ever put in an ASEAN document, especially given how seamlessly ASEAN had presented its history to this point (ASEAN 2006b: 2).

The theme continued with plans to upgrade the 'culture of commitment to honour and implement decisions, agreements and timelines' (ASEAN 2006b: 4). The report called for the establishment of dispute-settlement mechanisms 'in all fields of ASEAN cooperation', including compliance monitoring and enforcement mechanisms – in effect, sanctioning non-compliance in some form. It further called for an empowered ASEAN Secretariat engaged in monitoring compliance across all ASEAN agreements. The section on more effective decision-making noted that whilst the 'consensus style . . . has served ASEAN well and should be preserved as the guiding principle . . . [it] should aid, but not impede, ASEAN's cohesion and effectiveness' (ASEAN 2006b: 6). To this end, the report advocated the possibility of introducing both voting on certain decisions where consensus could not be achieved, and the creation of a more flexible approach to regionalism where sub-groups of ASEAN members could proceed in activities without allowing the reluctance of other members to block that activity.

The report outlined an ASEAN that stepped decisively away from its historical path towards a very different vision for regional cooperation. Indeed, it aimed explicitly at crafting an ASEAN Union, indicating that it clearly understood the regional situation as one requiring some sort of formal integration rather than ASEAN's traditionally lax coordination (David Martin Jones 2008: 737). The bold vision outlined by the report suggested a 'sea change in the thinking among ASEAN elites' (Caballero-Anthony 2008: 74). If enacted, this sea change would strike a death blow to the ASEAN that had evolved since 1967, and the broad consensus that any agreement would be weakly enforced and that states were free to violate even the most central of commitments when they felt it necessary. Three reasons lay behind this boldness. First, the report was only the first stage of a protracted process of finalising the ASEAN Charter, and was not going to be the final opportunity for states to have their say; it was not subject to the intense political jockeying that the final draft of the Charter would be. Second, the democratic members of ASEAN pushed strongly to have their voices heard and managed to overcome the default reluctance of other members (Sukma 2011: 113). This pulled the report away from ASEAN's traditional baseline consensus position towards something more agreeable to ASEAN's democratic members.[20] Third and finally, the composition of the EPG exacerbated the imbalance of the grouping. ASEAN's more democratic members sent retired but very senior political figures – Alatas from Indonesia, former Philippines President Fidel Ramos, and former Thai Deputy Prime Minister and Foreign Minister Kasemsamosorn Kasemsri. Whilst Vietnam also nominated former Deputy Prime Minister Nguyen Manh Cam, Laos sent a former Deputy Minister of Commerce, Cambodia an advisor to the Prime Minister, and Myanmar the Chair of the Civil Service Selection and Training Board. The asymmetry in the seniority of participants, and the social position of people such as Alatas in ASEAN's institutional history, enhanced the ability of democratic members to shape the report.

The boldness of the EPG was short-lived. The HLTF charged with turning the EPG report into a draft charter was explicitly told that the charter needed to be practical and doable, rather than a grandiose statement of a new ASEAN. Mely Caballero-Anthony (2008: 75) argues that the HLTF was 'apparently also instructed to exclude any discussions on sanctions and not to change the consensus decision-making process'. Rosario Gonzalez-Manalo (2009: 44), chair of the HLTF for a time, recorded that the taskforce displayed a 'general tendency to create a Charter that will keep the intergovernmental character of ASEAN and dispel any suggestion of creating a supra-national body'. This tendency was unsurprising given that members of the HLTF were active figures in national foreign affairs ministries. The representatives of the CLMV states adhered together to 'protect' the traditional ASEAN approach, sometimes aided by Singapore and Malaysia who also sought to maintain firm control of domestic dissent, often where that dissent was pro-democratic in nature (Leviter 2010: 194). The result was a Charter that more closely matched the desires of ASEAN's less progressive members. Jusuf Wanandi, a leading figure in the Track II dialogues that surround ASEAN, said that 'the creation of the charter, for example, was mostly guided by ASEAN's new members' (quoted in Morada 2008: 45). As such it is unsurprising that the final Charter document was an almost complete restatement of the traditional ASEAN approach as reflected in Bali II and VAP, with very little of the original intensity of the EPG's report remaining.

---

[20] Democracies are more comfortable with external institutional commitments that concern their domestic policies and in particular that seek international recognition of democracy in order to prevent 'backsliding'. See Morlino (2004). This is especially the case for democratising countries. See Mansfield & Pevehouse (2006); Pevehouse (2002).

The preamble of the Charter includes the need to respect 'the fundamental importance of amity and cooperation, and the principles of sovereignty, equality, territorial integrity, non-interference, consensus and unity in diversity' (ASEAN 2007b: preamble). With that stated, the preamble then states that members should adhere 'to principles of democracy, the rule of law and good governance, respect for and protection of human rights and fundamental freedoms' (ASEAN 2007b: preamble). The juxtaposition of these claims – the earlier embedded historic principles and the latter (subservient given their positioning) newer commitments – carried on throughout the Charter. Article 1 enumerated ASEAN's purposes to 'maintain and enhance peace, security and stability' (1.1); ensuring that 'the peoples and Member States of ASEAN live in peace with the world at large in a just, democratic and harmonious environment' (1.4); to 'alleviate poverty and narrow the development gap' (1.6); to 'strengthen democracy, enhance good governance and the rule of law, and to promote and protect human rights and fundamental freedoms, with due regard to the rights and responsibilities' of members (1.7). Article 2 lists ASEAN's guiding principles, and endorses all previous ASEAN 'declarations, agreements, conventions, concords, treaties and other instruments' (ASEAN 2007b: article 2). With that in place, article 2 continues with a call for ASEAN and its members to act in accordance with principles as diverse as respect for the independence, sovereignty, equality, territorial integrity, and national identity of all members; non-interference in the internal affairs of members; freedom from external interference, subversion, and coercion; adherence to the rule of law, good governance, the principles of democracy, and constitutional government; respect for fundamental freedoms, the promotion and protection of human rights, and the promotion of social justice; and abstention from participating in any policy which threatens the sovereignty, territorial integrity, or political and economic stability of ASEAN members (ASEAN 2007b).

Beyond aims and principles, the Charter finalised a range of institutional matters. ASEAN Summits were formalised as the 'supreme policy making body of ASEAN' and would now meet twice a year (ASEAN 2007b: article 7.2(a)), as would the ASEAN Coordinating Council, comprising foreign ministers. Each ASEAN Community would be headed by its own council, and underneath these sectoral ministerial bodies would meet as appropriate. Every ministerial-level meeting would be matched by senior officials meetings below them. A committee of permanent representatives would be formed, one from each member-state accorded ambassadorial rank, providing a constant coordination role. One of the few echoes of the EPG report was in the discussion of rules of procedure, where in the realm of economic commitments only 'a formula for flexible participation, including the ASEAN Minus X formula, may be applied where there is a consensus to do so' (ASEAN 2007b: article 21). The Charter, therefore, was not so much a reconciliation of the competing pressures on ASEAN as a final acceptance that the irreconcilability of these demands was no reason not to proceed with ASEAN reform. The Charter was a classic ASEAN document – it outlined a vision of ASEAN where tension within the principles it contained was imagined away in favour of a harmony that simply did not exist. The sleight of hand that came from representing the Charter as codifying existing practice was just part of the process of drawing the veil over the reality of a region whose practices did not live up to what was being claimed.

The ratification of the Charter, especially by the democratic states, who had pushed for the EPG report and were now accepting something less ambitious, illustrates two important points. First, there remained, forty years after its foundation, a deep diversity of views about what ASEAN was and should be. Second, democratic states remained willing to support ASEAN even when it fell short of their aspirations, and as a result ASEAN's baseline contribution to national and regional goals remained valued. This does not mean that the democratic states embraced the Charter; rather, they gritted their teeth and accepted it. For example, the Indonesian parliament was strongly and openly critical of the Charter. Jürgen Rüland identifies three reasons why this was the case. Materially, legislators were not convinced that the Charter provided much benefit to Indonesia. Normatively, the Charter was held to be a very weak expression of Indonesia's commitment to human rights and democracy. Procedurally, the Charter did very little to improve the decision-making systems of ASEAN or its ability to promote compliance (Rüland 2009: 382–5). Indonesia ratified the Charter, but only after a contentious debate and a framing of ratification as the beginning of a further process of refinement which would address Indonesian concerns.[21]

Three Vignettes of Contemporary ASEAN: Economics, Human Rights, and Myanmar

Since the Charter, ASEAN has been preoccupied with completing the community-building process through the launching of the ASEAN Community blueprints (one for each pillar) which detailed activities that needed to be completed by 2015, the declaration that the community was now 'created' in 2015, and the launch of Blueprint 2025 for the next stage of

---

[21] Academic debate at the time also emphasised that the Charter was very much an interim step towards something greater. See Tay (2008).

regionalism. To highlight the nature of ASEAN in this period, I present three short vignettes of regional cooperation – economics, human rights, and relations with Myanmar.

Economic cooperation has long been a centrepiece of ASEAN's regional project. The ASEAN Economic Community (AEC) was predicated on four components: a single market and production base, a competitive economic region, equitable economic development, and integration into the global economy whilst enhancing ASEAN centrality (ASEAN 2009a). Within each area a series of tasks and goals were outlined. Progress against these targets was initially measured through a scorecard system where member-states would self-report progress to the ASEAN Secretariat. This mechanism resulted in the conclusion that 74.5 per cent of ASEAN's economic commitments were realised by 2012. As Jörn Dösch (2017) explains, however, this figure was hardly credible given that ASEAN stopped releasing the data which would have enabled verification. The AEC has struggled to make forward motion, reflecting the same 'hesitant pattern of regional collaboration' shown elsewhere in ASEAN's activities (Dösch 2017: 33). Non-tariff measures to limit international trade and protect domestic producers have thwarted the realisation of a true ASEAN single market even as tariff barriers to trade have fallen (Dösch 2017: 35). The impression given of the AEC by 2015 was one of ambition out-tracking reality, with member-states carefully engaging with the AEC for fear of jeopardising their own domestic political economies (Jones 2016).

In regard to human rights, the ASEAN Political-Security Community blueprint outlined the steps that ASEAN would take to promote and protect human rights (ASEAN 2009c: subsection A.1.5). These included following through on the commitment made in the ASEAN Charter to form a human rights body of some sort, augmented by a commitment to craft a terms of reference (ToR) for that body to guide its activities (ASEAN 2009c: 8). The body created was the ASEAN Intergovernmental Commission on Human Rights (AICHR) and its ToR illustrates the way that re-radicalising human rights could work even at the most granular level. The AICHR was tied to 'respect for the independence, sovereignty, equality, territorial integrity and national identity of all ASEAN Member States' as well as respect for 'non-interference' and 'the right of every Member State to lead its national existence free from external interference' (ASEAN 2009b: article 2). As such, it was framed explicitly as both inter-governmental – not at all supranational with its overtones of regional oversight of members – and consultative (ASEAN 2009b: article 3). The AICHR was provided with no power of oversight, no ability to investigate violations, and no right of individual petition. All AICHR decisions were to be reached through consensus. The ToR provided states in general, and the non-democratic members especially, complete control over the workings of the AICHR. This control was emphasised through the unlikely medium of the ASEAN Human Rights Declaration (AHRD). Drafted behind closed doors, the AHRD is in one dimension progressive – it includes commitments to advanced civil and political rights which are not present in many of the states who helped draft the document. At the same time, the declaration states that 'nothing in this declaration may be interpreted as implying for any state, group or person any right to perform any act aimed at undermining the purposes and principles of ASEAN' (ASEAN 2012a: article 40). Given that ASEAN's purposes and principles as outlined in the ASEAN Charter prioritise non-interference, sovereign equality, and domestic freedom, article 40 effectively undermines the promotion and protection of the standards outlined in the previous thirty-nine articles (Davies 2014a; Pisanò 2014; Renshaw 2013).

As noted previously, the ongoing and often worsening violations of human rights within ASEAN members illustrates the weakness of these regional commitments. But they also illustrate the dangers of ASEAN's community-building project when so much of that project no longer rests on even the thinnest of substantive agreement. In 2004, Philippines Foreign Minister Alberto Romulo argued that the goals of inter-state peace and security were 'dependent on one crucial issue ... the protection and promotion of human rights across the region' (quoted in Hadi 2006: 6). ASEAN Secretary-General Ong Keng Yong (2004) similarly noted that the ASEAN Community 'could not become a reality if we did not first build cohesive and caring communities'. These claims were ignored when in 2015, ASEAN declared the ASEAN Community to be complete, despite systematic failings of its human rights architecture. This was more significant than just another example of ASEAN's enduring compliance gap. The engagement with human rights came about because of the desire to make ASEAN appear to be a caring organisation, but it was only possible to get agreement from all members by diluting those commitments almost entirely. Yet in doing so the resulting regional architecture is exposed to widespread criticism and legitimacy deficits, the very shortcomings that the process was initiated to avoid. The hypocrisy of early ASEAN was limited to the elite who chose to overlook it. The hypocrisy of today's ASEAN is known widely to the public, with serious consequences for their engagement with the regional project.

The relationship between Myanmar and ASEAN during the 2000s demonstrates how far ASEAN members could deviate from norms of non-interference if pressed to do so and, simultaneously, how uncomfortable it was when these deviations were open to public scrutiny. From 1988 to 2011, Myanmar was ruled either overtly or behind-the-scenes by the military. Throughout this period, Myanmar's governance was characterised by systematic violence and abrogation of the rule of law. Prominent examples of this repression included the repeated detention of Aung Sun Suu Kyi, and the 2007 violent crackdown of the Saffron Revolution. The actions of Myanmar's military junta during the early and mid-2000s caused international condemnation and mounting pressure on ASEAN to 'do something' about its most wayward member. Myanmar was in clear violation of ASEAN's growing, on-paper, commitments to human rights, democracy, good governance, and human-centric development. Yet translating this violation into commonly agreed action was very difficult; ASEAN's response ultimately amounted to a combination of strongly worded statements and wishful thinking that something would happen. In the communiqués of the AMM, ASEAN expressed mounting concern in the late 2000s about the situation in Myanmar, calling for democratisation and the freeing of political prisoners (see overview in Davies 2012, 2018; Emmerson 2008). After the Saffron Revolution crackdown, individual ASEAN members, such as Singapore, noted their revulsion at Myanmar's activities (Pereira 2007). It is difficult to say that these statements are anything other than a form of interference in the domestic affairs of an ASEAN member (Davies 2014b). Yet the closest ASEAN ever got to formally punishing Myanmar was to pressure it to relinquish the chair of ASEAN in 2005. Throughout this period, Myanmar retained full membership rights and participated in the processes of regional reform, including drafting the Charter and its commitments to human rights and democracy, whilst at the same time violating those standards with apparent impunity.

Since 2010 Myanmar has moved towards democratisation, although given the preponderant role that the military still plays in the political, social, and economic life of the country it cannot be classified as an embedded democratic system (see the discussion of embedded democracy and its characteristics in Merkel 2004). The 2010 elections, which were held by the international community as not having met standards of democratic rigour or transparency, were warmly welcomed by ASEAN and marked the end of ASEAN's weak public engagement with Myanmar's domestic political situation.[22] This silence continued throughout the ongoing Rohingya crisis (Cheesman 2017). The Rohingya, a minority in Rakhine State bordering Bangladesh, have been denied citizenship of Myanmar and are viewed as economic migrants. Myanmar's central government, both before and after the apparent democratic

---

[22] Compare the United Nations Secretary-General's response in United Nations (2010) with that of Vietnam in its role as chair of ASEAN (TalkVietnam 2010).

transition, has followed a policy of extreme repression and violence that has seen accusations of ethnic cleansing and even genocide and large-scale refugee outflows as desperate Rohingya flee the country. ASEAN's official position on the Rohingya crisis can be summed up in one word: silence. When thousands of Rohingya refugees were at sea in mid-2015 searching for a place to land, ASEAN was excluded from a regional meeting on the issue. ASEAN made no comment on the situation, and when the issue returned to international prominence in 2017 with another Myanmar crackdown (with Aung Sun Suu Kyi playing a leading role given her position as the first State Counsellor of Myanmar), ASEAN again remained silent. This silence is in contrast to some ASEAN members, notably Malaysia, whose prime minister openly called the situation a genocide and urged the world to 'act' to address it (Associated Press 2016).

3.2 Holding It All Together: Ritualised Unity as Public Performance

Given the shift towards phantom regionalism, what kept ASEAN together? Two factors are important in explaining ASEAN's endurance. First is the 'public face' that the organisation has tried to create through fostering an ASEAN identity and the development of ASEAN's symbols, and second is the increasing sophistication of ASEAN's ritual life.

ASEAN has increased its efforts to present itself to the regional public by developing symbols. Before 1997, ASEAN was already engaged in developing a greater sense of belonging to the regional project for its member-state populations. After 1997, this activity sharpened as ASEAN sought to protect itself from public criticism. In VAP, a section is dedicated to promoting an ASEAN identity, noting that amidst the diversity of the region there were also unifying experiences of history, geography, and aspiration (ASEAN 2004: paragraph 3.4). The EPG report on the ASEAN Charter, true to its status as one of ASEAN's most progressive documents, spoke of improving the ASEAN identity as a way to shed ASEAN's 'image of being an elitist organisation comprising exclusively diplomats and government officials' (ASEAN 2006b). The report recommended ongoing consultation with civil society, business, and academic institutions as a way to provide substance to ASEAN's people-oriented regionalism. It recommended activities to cement the commemoration of ASEAN into people's daily lives, suggesting such things as emphasising ASEAN Day (8 August), as well as enhanced regional activity in the spheres of culture, sports, art, heritage, museums, exhibitions, and youth activities. The report also recommended that ASEAN clearly represent itself through the traditional symbols of politics – 'ASEAN shall have a flag, emblem, anthem and motto' (ASEAN 2006b: paragraph 48).

These symbols were endorsed in Chapter XI of the ASEAN Charter. Although Chapter XI is rarely spoken about, given our focus on ritualised regionalism, it is worthy of attention. ASEAN's motto was established as 'One Vision, One Identity, One Community', which now emblazons the front page of most ASEAN documentation and is projected on screens and backdrops at ASEAN's public events. Although the above discussion indicates strongly that there were multiple visions of ASEAN, very little common identity, and a great reluctance to act as a community, this reality matters little in the face of the creative representation of regionalism. The ASEAN emblem, ten stalks of rice bound together, has a very clear set of symbolic meanings (see Image 3.1). The emblem 'represents a stable, peaceful, united and dynamic ASEAN', and the colours – blue, red, white, and yellow – represent 'the main colours of the state crests of all the ASEAN Member States . . . The blue represents peace and stability. Red depicts courage and dynamism, white shows purity and yellow symbolises prosperity' (ASEAN no date b). The bound rice stalks 'represent the dream of ASEAN's Founding Fathers for an ASEAN comprising all the countries in Southeast Asia, bound together in friendship and solidarity' (ASEAN no date b). The enclosing circle 'represents the unity of ASEAN' (ASEAN no date b). The emblem is to be used in all ASEAN official activities, with member-states encouraged to use the emblem in any function that relates to ASEAN. Interestingly, the emblem is 'not to be used for political purposes' (ASEAN no date b). However, symbols are quintessentially political objects – their purpose is to project a particular image and generate a particular senti-ment. De-politicisation in this context is evidence of its political role as it stands as an attempt to place the emblem and its messages above debate.

The ASEAN anthem, 'an expression of ASEAN unity', should be played at ASEAN formal meetings and related events, and to commemorate special occasions:

> Raise our flag high, sky high
> Embrace the pride in our heart
> ASEAN we are bonded as one
> Look-in out to the world.
> For peace, our goal from the very start
> And prosperity to last.
> We dare to dream we care to share.
> Together for ASEAN
> we dare to dream,
> we care to share for it's the way of ASEAN (ASEAN no date a).

It is easy to be flippant about the wording, but in its repeated public usage, like all anthems it can also be seen as an effort to bind together the people and the institution. A similar situation occurs with the flag, which is ASEAN's emblem centred on a blue background. ASEAN has created strict guidelines for the usage of the flag, revealing its symbolic importance (ASEAN no date c).

The creation of these symbols of unity, and the construction of ritual around their usage, mark both an increase in the sophistication of ASEAN's self-representation and an effort to expand that representation to the wider ASEAN public in line with the goal of people-centred regionalism.[23] Given this is ASEAN, the representation of ASEAN as people-centred was not accompanied by the reality of people-centricity. The EPG report on the ASEAN Charter had called for the full integration of civil society actors into ASEAN's framework. Yet this has not come to pass. ASEAN elites have been comfortable using civil society as a conduit through which to make ASEAN better known, but have proven largely unwilling to actually allow civil society substantive input into the creation and running of ASEAN commitments and institutions (Collins 2008: 328). Civil society actors, unable to engage with ASEAN directly, have focused their efforts on 'created spaces' alongside ASEAN's formal structures as a way to influence the region (Gerard 2014, 2015). There are two sides to this engagement with civil society actors. Gerard is sceptical of their ability to influence ASEAN, highlighting the ineffectiveness of their strategies of organising parallel conferences alongside ASEAN official events and protests to attract opinion (2014: 282), and that as a result ASEAN's 'people-centredness' was lacking. Alternately, the growth and endurance of regional civil society even in created spaces suggests that ASEAN's rhetorical focus on people-centricity created the permissive conditions for some sort of regional activity to develop where previously there were none. If we step away from assuming that ASEAN is synonymous with Southeast Asia and, instead, is part of a broader array of actors and processes within the region, such civil society activity supports the claim that the region, as a whole, is making progress towards people-centredness even if ASEAN itself is moving more slowly in that direction.

The increasing number of ASEAN symbols are embedded in the sophistication and standardisation of ASEAN's ritual life, culminating in the strict *Guide to ASEAN Practices and Protocol*. To illustrate this trend towards standardisation and repetition, I focus on one dimension where rituals and symbols come together – the photographic representation of ASEAN meetings. ASEAN's

---

[23] Simon Creak's (2010, 2017) work on the role of sport in Southeast Asia, particularly the Southeast Asian Games, reveals the coexistence of unifying rituals and symbols between the countries and peoples of Southeast Asia and sustained disunity and self-interest.

guidelines for photography at all events are carefully scripted in the *Guide*, which outlines the approach for photography at ASEAN Summits, meetings with Dialogue Partners, ASEAN+3, the East Asia Summit, the ASEAN Coordinating Council, Opening Ceremonies, Senior Officials Meetings, External Partners, Sectoral Partners, the ASEAN Regional Forum (ARF) and for the presentation of credentials by Ambassadors to ASEAN (ASEAN 2015). For each, the arrangement of participants and the location of national and ASEAN flags are specified. Elsewhere in the *Guide*, each of these events has its backdrop specified. For example, every ASEAN Summit has the same format:

> The backdrop of the Summit shall bear the chairmanship logo, ASEAN emblem (if not reflected in the chairmanship logo), title and theme of the chairmanship, date and name of the venue city, town or place where the Summit is being held as illustrated in Diagram 1. If the Summit is held in a place other than a government premise such as a hotel, the name of the hotel should not be included in the backdrop.
>
> The arrangement of the flags of ASEAN Member States will be in alphabetical order with five flags on both sides of the stage. The ASEAN flag shall flank the ASEAN Member States' flags on the extreme right side of the stage (ASEAN 2015: 3; see also the images in ASEAN Secretariat 2016).

This standardisation has replaced what was a more varied and haphazard approach. Early summits showed a wide variety of arrangements of leaders, with different backgrounds and ways in which those leaders stood and related to one another in the space (see ASEAN 2012b for photographic representation of early ASEAN Summits). At the 6th Summit in Ha Noi in 1998, leaders grasp hands above their heads. At the 7th Summit in Brunei Seri Begawan, some leaders are linking arms across their bodies whilst others are interlocking their elbows, resulting in a rather disharmonious presentation. At the 9th and 10th Summits (Bali and Vientiane respectively) leaders stand face-on to the camera with their arms by their sides. By the 13th ASEAN Summit, held in Singapore, all heads of state lined up holding hands with those standing next to them, with their arms crossed in front of their bodies. This approach has now become standard for all ASEAN-led meetings.[24]

Standardisation and repetition serves two crucial purposes in today's ASEAN. First, it locks the participants into a performance of unity. Twice a year, heads of state and government come together and perform a highly choreographed ritual where symbols of unity and harmony are reified, and

---

[24] The ASEAN Secretariat's Flickr homepage provides a wealth of photos demonstrating the standardized visual representation that has developed. See www.flickr.com/photos/aseansecretariat/

where the participants partake in a demonstration of respect for those symbols and one another. ASEAN unity, harmony, and control are directly experienced by political elites, before the moment passes, the cameras are turned off, and they return to arguing about their national interests. These moments are sacred ASEAN spaces and experiences. The second purpose is presentational – the beatific smiles of elites in front of a fixed and familiar backdrop convey to audiences the sense of control and continuity. Not only do ASEAN leaders participate in these ritual moments directly, but also the reproduction of these images in newspapers and online exposes these moments to a wider audience. In this way, ASEAN demonstrates its utility and relevance, as well as its own peculiar form of people-centricity.

3.3 ASEAN in the Asia-Pacific

ASEAN continued to develop its engagement with the wider Asia-Pacific, through the ARF and by developing other mechanisms. These mechanisms have followed similar paths inasmuch as each has expanded from narrow discussions of political and security issues into wider discussions about economic, social, and political goals. Each mechanism is also accompanied by significant scepticism.

The ARF continued in its gradualist approach, although as noted above, it remains stuck in its first phase of confidence-building, without progressing to a substantive preventative diplomacy agenda.[25] The ARF has excelled in offering an enduring forum for an ever-wider range of conversations involving the majority of leading states and actors in global politics. ASEAN+3 was launched in December 1997 with an informal meeting of leaders of ASEAN and Japan, China, and South Korea. The grouping, smaller than the ARF which preceded it and the East Asia Summit process which came later, was exclusively East Asian, and excluded the United States. ASEAN+3 was framed as 'the main vehicle towards the long-term goal of building an East Asian Community, with ASEAN as the driving force' (ASEAN 2017b). ASEAN+3 has become rapidly institutionalised and now includes meetings of heads of state, senior ministers, and senior officials to discuss issues as diverse as health, labour, tourism, energy, drug trafficking, agriculture, and communication (Ba 2009: 214–16). The East Asia Summit, launched in 2005 with ASEAN nominally in the lead, was smaller than the ARF and brought together the heads of state and government of leading Asia-Pacific states.[26] Hopes were high that the

---

[25] An overview of the ARF's first two decades, together with key documents, can be found in ASEAN Secretariat (2014).

[26] Founding members included all ASEAN countries, Australia, China, India, Japan, New Zealand, and South Korea. The United States and Russia joined in 2011.

East Asia Summit would provide new impetus to Asia-Pacific regionalism (Malik 2006: 207). However, the reality has been less impressive, and the region's tensions have continued to worsen as China rises, the US falters, and North Korea festers. The scale and complexity of these trends and challenges is daunting. ASEAN's failure is less damning than it might otherwise be, but it is hard to argue that the East Asia Summit, or any of ASEAN's other external activities, have transformed the region.

The emerging theme with which ASEAN chose to label its external relations was centrality – ASEAN would be central to the provision of Asia-Pacific security. 'Centrality' did not appear in Vision 2020, the Hanoi Plan of Action, Bali II, or VAP, but does appear in the 2006 EPG report on the ASEAN Charter, and from then with regularity. ASEAN centrality appears repeatedly in the AMM joint communiqués from 2006, and in the ASEAN Summits from 2007. It emerged, however, fully formed, as ASEAN was not aiming to establish its centrality so much as to 'retain its centrality' (ASEAN 2006b: article 51), uphold its centrality (ASEAN 2007a), or 'maintain [it] on the context of ASEAN related regional architectures' (ASEAN 2006a). 'Centrality' denoted a return to the optimism of the late 1990s and was not a new concept (Acharya 2017: 273), but it spoke of ASEAN's permanence, success, and leadership in the Asia-Pacific. Yet centrality, and its repeated usage and presentation as something that already exists, did not represent reality. The ARF continued to flounder, stuck in its initial phase of confidence-building without ever having progressed to preventative diplomacy (Emmers & Tang 2012: 89).

ASEAN's external efforts have, just like ASEAN itself, a chimerical quality. On paper, ASEAN presents itself as driving Asia-Pacific security, yet in reality as a collection of small powers or in the case of Indonesia a potential great power of the future, ASEAN has very limited ability to directly shape the interests of China or the United States. ASEAN's efforts at centrality can easily be framed as the product of the great powers and their own interests in using ASEAN centrality as a convenient façade rather than ASEAN's ability to lead (Acharya 2017: 273–4). Those who value enduring conversations and believe that at the very least states should continue to talk to each other tend to value ASEAN's external engagements, and those who hunt for real-world examples of ASEAN 'providing measurable benefit' to Asia-Pacific peace and security tend to question it. Viewed together, ASEAN's external activities have helped bring states together in discussion, but have led to very little substantive progress beyond that, with the power tensions and alliance politics playing out within these institutions rather than being resolved by them (Goh 2018).

It is worth asking why ASEAN as an institution, and as member-states individually, bothers with these activities? There is nothing pre-ordained or required of them. We should be suspicious of claims that all ASEAN members sought to socialise norms of non-interference/intervention widely given their own internal approach to those values. More persuasively, ASEAN's external engagement is a product of ASEAN's weakness. Throughout its history, ASEAN's successes or failures have been the product of the situation beyond Southeast Asia – US policy in the 1960s, the Cold War in the 1970s and 1980s, the end of the Cold War in the 1990s and Western democratic triumphalism, the travails of the global economy, and most recently a rising China. ASEAN's ability to perform and represent unity in Southeast Asia is predicated on a broadly conducive international setting – when external challenges mount, and when great powers jostle, ASEAN is well aware that it loses out. Most importantly, external tensions exacerbate internal tensions which make the plausibility of ASEAN's theatre all the more difficult. We have seen this in the tensions generated by Cambodia's close relationship with China which, for the first time, led to an inability to release a joint communiqué for the AMM held in Phnom Penh in 2012. Cambodia refused to allow language in the document that was strongly critical of China's position in the South China Sea. The situation was nearly repeated in 2016 when Cambodia again came close to blocking the Vientiane AMM's joint communiqué. The situation was only resolved following a considerable backdown by other ASEAN members (Parameswaran 2016).

3.4 ASEAN at Fifty

ASEAN's experiences of crisis and reform have changed the expression of regionalism in Southeast Asia. The remit of regionalism expanded across new areas of governance and the institutional sophistication of ASEAN increased as a result – there were now more meetings, more often, about a greater number of things. This evolution had come about as ASEAN came to specify the meaning of caring communities and the regional role in that process. This process was characterised by deep disagreement between member-states and a sense of confusion about what to do. Into this confusion, norm entrepreneurs and more liberal ASEAN members proposed certain solutions that moved ASEAN towards democracy and good governance. These commitments were accepted only after being traditionalised and de-radicalised through the invoking of ASEAN's symbols. Past treaties, declarations, and statements were imported wholesale into new situations. This act of importation both reassured member-states as to the maintenance of the traditional approach to regional affairs, and defused the potential radicalism of engaging with 'people-centricity'. The result was an increase in the incoherence of ASEAN as a regional organisation, where its aims increasingly conflicted with each other, and where its approach to regional governance retarded the realisation of many of its own goals. In turn, this reform shifted the regional project towards a 'phantom regionalism' where the region as presented in the treaties, declarations, and work plans of ASEAN was no longer something that all member-states wished to see come to pass.

This shift, at least to date, has not imperilled ASEAN's existence. The continued relevance of ASEAN comes from the continuity of ASEAN's overarching purpose. There remained a consistent prioritisation of ASEAN as a reassurance vehicle of national freedom through the defence of domestic sovereign prerogatives. These freedoms continued to include the right to violate regional norms of non-interference. Because the intention did not change, the truth of ASEAN also remained constant – there were no deeply shared norms outlining common views of legitimate behaviour that bound together the ten members. This incoherence, and the threats it posed to member-state freedom, was kept in check not through being confronted and reconciled, but in the stoic refusal to officially acknowledge its existence. As ASEAN changed, and yet did not change, ritual became ever more important to demonstrating ASEAN unity in the absence of any unifying principles beyond independence. It is no coincidence that ASEAN has come to possess a robust set of symbols, and that its public events became more numerous and more ritualised. These oft-overlooked dimensions of ASEAN regionalism were vital acts of reassurance and representation of regional unity; reassuring ASEAN elites and extending ASEAN into a people-oriented but still elitist institution.

4 Choosing Regionalism

It is all too easy to assume that 'the region' was, and remains, an automatic and unthinking choice, and that ASEAN was destined to endure and was set on a straight path towards its current design. These assumptions are faulty. As the previous discussion has shown, ASEAN was repeatedly chosen by elites as a worthwhile investment of time, resources, and political capital. At its creation in 1967, ASEAN was launched as a statement of intent shared by five states whose relations were characterised by suspicion. The intent behind the words of the Bangkok Declaration was clear – that coexistence and the establishment of some sort of reliable peace in Southeast Asia was the *sine qua non* for their other goals, be they domestic, political, or geostrategic in nature. The failure of trans-regional efforts such as Bandung, the continuing tension between reliance on Western powers for security whilst also seeking to chart an independent course, and the collapse of previous efforts at Southeast Asian regionalism all shaped the nascent ASEAN. ASEAN would be a vehicle of reassurance not one of integration – it would defend and promote sovereignty, not curtail its enjoyment. Over time, buffeted by external circumstances, shifting values, and their own evolving political priorities, Southeast Asian states have continued to choose ASEAN. The economic growth of the region in the 1970s and 1980s, coupled with the need to handle the consequences of Vietnam's invasion of Cambodia, allowed ASEAN to become more institutionally sophisticated and vocal. In the post–Cold War world, ASEAN was again chosen, this time as a way to ensure that key commitments to sovereignty and member-state independence were not eroded in a post-communist world. In the aftermath of the Asian financial crisis, ASEAN was felt to be the appropriate vehicle within which to express a regional concern with the lives of those living in member states.

At the confluence of the competing pressures on regionalism, the challenges faced, and the choice to recommit to ASEAN, patterns of institutional reform emerged – the slow accretion of functions before 1997, the partial discontinuity of the financial crisis, and the rapid but path-dependent reforms since the early 2000s. ASEAN leaders had to improvise as different issues arose. Part of the process of this improvisation has been the growing complexity of the regional body. The early coherence of ASEAN, and the way its aims, institutions, and practices aligned around an illiberal vision of authoritarianism were predicated on social stability and economic growth. After 1997 this vision was challenged but ultimately not overturned. Instead newer ideas about social welfare, economics, and even civil and political rights were brought into ASEAN, but only alongside existing, more traditional, ideas. The result has been that today, in its institutional form, ASEAN's aspirations and practices are incoherent because different parts of its key documents now outline very different visions for ASEAN. I have sought to capture this shift by explaining it as a transition from ideal regionalism – where all could agree on the end-goals if not on progress towards them – to phantom regionalism, where the end-goals seem not to enjoy even token support.

Throughout these intertwined processes of choosing the region, and redesigning the regional organisation, an important constant emerges. Throughout ASEAN's history, the gap between 'on-paper' commitment and the actual practice of members has endured. This has been the case in relation to the hard issues of democracy promotion and the painful choices around economic integration and opening up domestic markets, and has also been true for the most foundational of ASEAN's commitments to non-intervention and freedom from external interference. This compliance gap illuminates the central conundrums of ASEAN – what and how has ASEAN actually achieved, and what benefit does the organisation bring to regional affairs? As indicated in the foregoing discussions, I do not think that ASEAN's new commitments are completely useless, although I have argued that their utility lies largely in other actors' use and mobilisation of them, not in their innate value or efficiency (Davies 2017a).

ASEAN has been successful in securing a particular type of regional peace and security – a peace of elites and a security of states. This feat is remarkable because it is so hard to see how the region in 1967 could have avoided inter-state war, and valuable because the region's undeniable progress since 1967 has been predicated on that peace. Yet at the heart of the regional project lies an emptiness, and the wisdom of ASEAN is that it has managed this emptiness rather than been consumed by it. Beyond the desire to maintain and improve the enjoyment of national freedom, very little unified the original or current members. At the heart of ASEAN's approach to regionalism has been the development of practices that manage these basic disagreements by accepting them as inevitable and working to contain their negative consequences. Sovereignty, non-intervention, non-interference, consensus, and unity have become key to the region, but less as shared values and more as common aspirations; they outline an ideal end-state to which all can agree. The fundamental commitment to national freedom is the root cause of this – freedom includes the right to interfere and intervene. Were this freedom to exist in limitless form, the regional stability that members wished for in order to pursue other goals would be undermined. Here lies the irreconcilable tension at the heart of all that ASEAN does.

The management of this tension between freedom to, and restrictions on, intervention and interference has been facilitated through the evolution of a ritual and symbolic life. Ritualised meetings and symbols of unity present the image of a region at peace with itself and bound together by the shared values that are outlined in so many of ASEAN's documents. They present something that is untrue, but no less of a unifier because of it. The process of ritualisation can be dated to the very start of ASEAN, and it accelerated via the increased number of ASEAN meetings and the language used to describe those meetings. Over time, key documents were crafted that became symbolic of this ideal vision of the region – the Treaty of Amity and Cooperation (TAC) especially, but also the Zone of Peace, Freedom and Neutrality and the ASEAN Charter. This latter document was referenced and repeated, and became centrally important as a vision of the region to which all could pay homage and, permitted by that act of homage, which all could violate when necessary. Post-1997 these moments of ritual, and the symbols surrounding these moments, have become more prominent. The *Guide to ASEAN's Practices and Protocol* that this work opened with illustrates the degree to which stagecraft, presentation, and symbols are tied together in the performance of unity. The rituals and symbols of ASEAN held in check the centrifugal tendencies of power politics by presenting the idea of a region that did not exist, and by persuading key elites to act as if it did exist at key performative moments, aligning practitioners with a vision of the past and the present and serving to frame the future as predictable and reassuring. These rituals did not, and could not, transform the region into something for which its most ardent supporters might wish, but they have been sufficient to hold in check the worst tendencies which its opponents so often see. Beyond the role of rituals and symbols explaining the presence and nature of regional peace and security, I have also argued that symbols have helped ease the path of regional reform. Key documents, again most often TAC, have become important ways in which ASEAN elites have approached questions of change. Change was impossible when it contradicted TAC; aligning change with TAC became the key to moving an issue forward.

4.1 ASEAN's New Challenges

The challenges that ASEAN faces today are the consequences of its approach to regional affairs and the diversity amongst its members. With a rising China, a declining US, and its own members re-evaluating both their foreign policy goals and mutual relationships, questions about the value of ASEAN for its members are pressing. Four key challenges stand out. The first challenge is internal. As Bilahari Kausikan (2017), Singapore's Ambassador at Large, remarked at a 2017 Roundtable on ASEAN at 50 organised by the ISEAS–Yusof Ishak Institute: 'the domestic political environments of several ASEAN members have become more complicated . . . not every new member has internalised the need for balance between national and regional interests as did the original members'. Kausikan focused on how countries such as Cambodia have, in placing their own national interest ahead of the regional, imperilled ASEAN's unity. Kausikan's take is particularly interesting as he is not pining for a lost ASEAN golden age of unity and agreement. He notes that national interests are always important, that consensus is not always achieved, and that the diversity of ASEAN's members means that ASEAN members will always have diverging national interests. Kausikan's concern, instead, is that many new members see no value in the regional dimension of their external relations when it conflicts with their own national interests. This is the real internal challenge, because if members refuse to see any value in ASEAN regionalism relative to their own desires, then there is no space for ASEAN's approach to regionalism to operate. The viability of the ritualised approach to regionalism rests on the constant balancing of national interests – the national interest was served by working through a region whose displays of unity permitted and managed diverging national interest.

Simultaneous with the potential for 'disengagement' with ASEAN by its members is the second challenge, that of the threat of ASEAN being misunderstood, either by its members or other actors, be they dialogue partners, civil society players, or even individuals. The 'on-paper' ASEAN conveys the impression of a regional organisation very different from its reality. This mismatch, in turn, raises expectations that are unlikely to be met. The scorn with which the ASEAN Human Rights Declaration was met by civil society within Southeast Asia (see Human Rights Watch 2012) exposed ASEAN to more pointed criticism because its failure could now be judged against its expressed commitments, not those of a third party. A very similar story can be told regarding the plight of the Rohingya people who, if ASEAN wants to be people-centred, need to be helped. Yet because of Myanmar's dual role as a full member of ASEAN and the very cause of the Rohingya refugees' plight, ASEAN is unable to assist. ASEAN is trapped and judged against standards which it created but cannot enforce. Whether ASEAN will work towards living up to its commitments or retain its traditional disinterest in compliance will shape how it is perceived and valued.

The alignment of national interests between some ASEAN members is a third challenge to the region. The above discussion has shown how in realms as diverse as economics, human rights, trade, security, and defence policy, ASEAN members may have little in common, but they often have a lot in common with a few of their ASEAN peers. There is no automatic reason why regional cooperation can only be expressed through ASEAN – it is simply the case that until now, ASEAN has been the only expression of regionalism in Southeast Asia. Fraying engagement with ASEAN because of disappointment in its defence of democracy (or concern that there is too much of a commitment), or disinterest in its economic plans and agreements, or the obstinacy of newer members, all threaten the emergence of sub-regional initiatives. To date, these have focused on sub-regional cooperation in areas such as piracy and security of the Malacca Strait, but there is no reason why this sub-regionalism should not expand. Whilst there is nothing necessarily problematic about the coexistence of more formalised sub-regional groupings alongside ASEAN, they at the very least problematise claims to ASEAN centrality and, inherently, undercut claims to ASEAN unity in a very public way.

The final challenge is external. ASEAN was and remains a collection of comparatively less powerful states. Even Indonesia is a long way from great power status. ASEAN has always faced external challenges; even during the broad predictability of the Cold War there were constant if shifting threats. Now the broader Indo-Pacific security order is under unprecedented challenge. A rising China has called into question the role of the US and its underpinning of the security architecture of the region, exacerbated by the election of President Donald J. Trump. In turn, this rise is exposing the fault lines within ASEAN – its inability to coherently defend member-state sovereign claims in the South China Sea, Cambodia's role as a Chinese proxy within ASEAN, and diverging responses to a declining US. ASEAN is entering a period where past certainties are being replaced by an endemic ambiguity. These ambiguities undercut ASEAN's already weak leadership role in the Asia-Pacific institutional architecture (Cook & Bisley 2016).

4.2 Final Words

In 1967, five states chose Southeast Asia as a meaningful conduit for the expression of their national interest. Their choice was wise. Learning from previous mistakes, ASEAN began as little more than a statement of intent. Through fifty turbulent years, it has developed from, and remained true to, its founding vision – a region of states defending their sovereignty and independence through joint action. Regional reform, whether driven by security concerns, norm contestation, or crises, has changed the expression of regionalism, making it both more sophisticated and more expansive. Yet none of these reforms have shaped a deep and enduring regional identity. ASEAN's acceptance and management of this absence is its greatest success whilst also, simultaneously, the cause of its enduring weakness. ASEAN's endurance over the last fifty years and the peace it has helped achieve means it is worthy of praise. Yet this praise must be qualified. ASEAN has failed to socialise many of the norms that are needed to fulfil its 'on-paper' vision. This failure is the inevitable consequence of its design and history.

Ultimately, regionalism is always a choice, and in Southeast Asia with its enduring diversities, it is especially so. In 1967, elites consciously chose to launch ASEAN, and at crucial times in its history elites have re-affirmed that choice with renewed attention to the regional project and the underlying decision that ASEAN was important to national goals. As regional and extra-regional tensions grow, new generations of political leaders, and the wider circle of public opinion, will need to again choose ASEAN. ASEAN's ritualised approach to regionalism has helped it endure and, in many ways, prosper.

Yet inherent in ritualism is the threat that it degenerates into something that becomes hollowed out as generations change and priorities shift. The challenge of managing competing national priorities and external great power politics, and maintaining an audience where ritual and symbol remain meaningful, is great. The challenge, however, is no less great than those that faced the region when five foreign ministers met in Bangkok and launched Southeast Asia on such an improbable journey.

Abbreviations

AEC	ASEAN Economic Community
AFTA	ASEAN Free Trade Area
AHRD	ASEAN Human Rights Declaration
AICHR	ASEAN Intergovernmental Commission on Human Rights
ARF	ASEAN Regional Forum
ASA	Association of Southeast Asia
AMM	Annual Ministerial Meeting
ASEAN	Association of Southeast Asian Nations
ASEAN+3	ASEAN plus China, Japan, and South Korea
CLMV	Cambodia, Laos, Myanmar, and Vietnam
EPG	Eminent Persons Group
HLTF	High-Level Task Force
IR	International Relations
PTA	preferential trade agreement
SEATO	Southeast Asia Treaty Organization
TAC	Treaty of Amity and Cooperation
ToR	terms of reference
UN	United Nations
VAP	Vientiane Action Programme
ZOPFAN	Zone of Peace, Freedom and Neutrality

References

Acharya, Amitav. (1997). Ideas, identity, and institution-building: From the 'ASEAN way' to the 'Asia-Pacific way'? *Pacific Review*, **10**(3), 319–46. doi:10.1080/09512749708719226.

(2001). *Constructing a Security Community in Southeast Asia: ASEAN and the Problem of Regional Order*, Abingdon: Routledge.

(2004). How ideas spread: Whose norms matter? Norm localization and institutional change in Asian regionalism. *International Organization*, **58**(2), 239–75. doi:10.1017/S0020818304582024.

(2005). Do norms and identity matter? Community and power in Southeast Asia's regional order. *Pacific Review*, **18**(1), 95–118. doi:10.1080/ 09512740500047199.

(2011). Dialogue and discovery: In search of international relations theories beyond the West. *Millennium: Journal of International Studies*, **39**(3), 619–37. doi:10.1177/0305829811406574.

(2017). The myth of ASEAN centrality? *Contemporary Southeast Asia*, **39**(2), 273–79.

Acharya, Amitav & Tan, See Seng. (2008). Introduction: The normative relevance of the Bandung conference for contemporary Asian and international order. In See Seng Tan and Amitav Acharya, eds., *Bandung Revisited: The Legacy of the 1955 Asian-African Conference for International Order*, Singapore: NUS Press, pp. 1–16.

Adler, Emanuel. (1997). Seizing the middle ground: Constructivism in world politics. *European Journal of International Relations*, 3(3), 319–63.

Ahmad, Zakaria Haji & Ghoshal, Baladas. (1999). The political future of ASEAN after the Asian crisis. *International Affairs*, **75**(4), 759–78.

Alagappa, Muthiah. (1993). Regionalism and the quest for security: ASEAN and the Cambodian conflict. *Journal of International Affairs*, **46**(2), 439–67.

ASEAN. (1967). The ASEAN Declaration (Bangkok Declaration) Bangkok, 8 August. asean.org/the-asean-declaration-bangkok-declaration-bangkok-8-august-1967/.

(1968). Joint Communiqué of the Second ASEAN Ministerial Meeting, Jakarta, 6–7 August. asean.org/?static_post=joint-communique-of-the-second-asean-ministerial-meeting-jakarta-6–7-august-1968.

(1969). Joint Communiqué of the Third ASEAN Ministerial Meeting, Cameron Highlands, 16–17 December. asean.org/?static_post=joint-com

munique-of-the-third-asean-ministerial-meeting-cameron-highlands-16–
17-december-1969.

(1971a). Joint Communiqué of the Fourth ASEAN Ministerial Meeting,
Manila, 12–13 March. asean.org/?static_post=joint-communique-of-the-
fourth-asean-ministerial-meeting-manila-12–13-march-1971.

(1971b). Zone of Peace, Freedom and Neutrality Declaration, 27 November.
www.icnl.org/research/library/files/Transnational/zone.pdf.

(1976a). Declaration of ASEAN Concord Adopted by the Heads of State/
Government at the 1st ASEAN Summit in Bali, Indonesia on 24
February. www.mfa.go.th/asean/contents/files/other-20130527–
163444-272383.pdf.

(1976b). Joint Communiqué of the First ASEAN Heads of Government
Meeting, Bali, 23–24 February. asean.org/?static_post=joint-communi
que-the-first-asean-heads-of-government-meeting-bali-23–24-february-
1976.

(1976c). Treaty of Amity and Cooperation in Southeast Asia, Indonesia,
February. asean.org/treaty-amity-cooperation-southeast-asia-indonesia-
24-february-1976/.

(1991). Joint Communiqué of the Twenty-Fourth ASEAN Ministerial
Meeting, Kuala Lumpur, 19–20 July. asean.org/?static_post=joint-commu
nique-of-the-twenty-fourth-asean-ministerial-meeting-kuala-lumpur-19–
20-july-1991.

(1992a). Joint Communiqué 25th ASEAN Ministerial Meeting, Manila,
Philippines, 21–22 July. asean.org/?static_post=joint-communique-25th-
asean-ministerial-meeting-manila-philippines-21–22-july-1992.

(1992b). Singapore Declaration of 1992, Singapore, 28 January. asean.org/?
static_post=singapore-declaration-of-1992-singapore-28-january-1992.

(1993). Joint Communiqué of the Twenty-Sixth ASEAN Ministerial
Meeting Singapore, 23–24 July. asean.org/?static_post=joint-communi
que-of-the-twenty-sixth-asean-ministerial-meeting-singapore-23–24-
july-1993.

(1994). Joint Communiqué of the Twenty-Seventh ASEAN Ministerial
Meeting, Bangkok, 22–23 July. asean.org/?static_post=joint-communi
que-of-the-twenty-seventh-asean-ministerial-meeting-bangkok-22–23-
july-1994.

(1995a). Bangkok Summit Declaration, 14–15 December. asean.org/?static_
post=bangkok-summit-declaration-of-1995-bangkok14-15-december-
1995.

(1995b). Joint Communiqué of the Twenty-Eighth ASEAN Ministerial
Meeting, Bandar Seri Begawan, 29–30 July. asean.org/?static_post=

joint-communique-of-the-twenty-eighth-asean-ministerial-meeting-ban
dar-seri-begawan-29–30-july-1995.

(1996). Joint Communiqué of the Twenty-Ninth ASEAN Ministerial
Meeting (AMM), Jakarta, 20–21 July. asean.org/?static_post=joint-com
munique-of-the-29th-asean-ministerial-meeting-amm-jakarta-20–21-
july-1996.

(1997). ASEAN Vision 2020, 15 December. asean.org/?static_post=asean-
vision-2020.

(2000). Report of the ASEAN Eminent Persons Group (EPG) on Vision
2020: The People's ASEAN. asean.org/?static_post=report-of-the-asean-
eminent-persons-group-epg-on-vision-2020-the-people-s-asean.

(2003). Declaration of ASEAN Concord II (Bali Concord II), 7 October.
asean.org/?static_post=declaration-of-asean-concord-ii-bali-concord-ii.

(2004). Vientiane Action Programme. www.asean.org/storage/images/
archive/VAP-10th%20ASEAN%20Summit.pdf.

(2005). Terms of Reference of the Eminent Persons Group (EPG) on the
ASEAN Charter. www.asean.org/wp-content/uploads/images/archive/
ACP-TOR.pdf.

(2006a). Joint Communiqué of the 39th ASEAN Ministerial Meeting
(AMM), Kuala Lumpur, 25 July. asean.org/?static_post=joint-communi
que-of-the-39th-asean-ministerial-meeting-amm-kuala-lumpur-25-july-
2006–3.

(2006b). Report of the Eminent Persons Group on the ASEAN Charter,
December. www.asean.org/wp-content/uploads/images/archive/19247.pdf.

(2007a). Chairperson's Statement of the 12th ASEAN Summit H. E. the
President Gloria Macapagal-Arroyo: One Caring and Sharing
Community, 13 January. asean.org/?static_post=chairperson-s-state
ment-of-the-12th-asean-summit-he-the-president-gloria-macapagal-
arroyo-one-caring-and-sharing-community.

(2007b). The ASEAN Charter, ASEAN Secretariat: Jakarta, 20 November.

(2009a). ASEAN Economic Community Blueprint. In *Roadmap for an ASEAN
Community: 2009–2015*, Jakarta: ASEAN Secretariat, pp. 21–40. www
.asean.org/storage/images/ASEAN_RTK_2014/2_Roadmap_for_ASEAN_
Community_20092015.pdf.

(2009b). ASEAN Intergovernmental Commission on Human Rights (Terms
of Reference), Jakarta: ASEAN Secretariat, October. aichr.org/?
dl_name=TOR-of-AICHR.pdf.

(2009c). ASEAN Political-Security Community Blueprint. In *Roadmap
for an ASEAN Community: 2009–2015*, Jakarta: ASEAN Secretariat, pp.
5–19.

(2012a). ASEAN Human Rights Declaration and the Phnom Penh Statement on the Adoption of the ASEAN Human Rights Declaration (AHRD), Jakarta: ASEAN Secretariat. www.asean.org/storage/images/ASEAN_RTK_2014/6_AHRD_Booklet.pdf.

(2012b). ASEAN Summits Photos, 24 July. asean.org/?static_post=asean-summits-photos.

(2015). *Guide to ASEAN Practices and Protocol*, Jakarta: ASEAN Secretariat, November. www.asean.org/storage/2015/11/publication/Guide_to_ASEAN_Practices_and_Protocol.pdf.

(2017a). Indicative ASEAN Notional Calendar 2017, 10 May. asean.org/storage/2015/05/ASEAN-Notional-Calendar-ASEC-Format-as-of-10-May-2017.pdf.

(2017b). Overview of ASEAN Plus Three Cooperation, June. asean.org/storage/2017/06/Overview-of-APT-Cooperation-Jun-2017.pdf.

(no date a). ASEAN Anthem. asean.org/asean/about-asean/asean-anthem/.

(no date b). ASEAN Emblem. asean.org/asean/about-asean/asean-emblem/.

(no date c). ASEAN Flag. asean.org/asean/about-asean/asean-flag/.

ASEAN Secretariat. (no date d). The ASEAN Regional Forum: A concept paper. aseanregionalforum.asean.org/library/arf-chairmans-statements-and-reports.html?id=132.

(1994). Chairman's Statement of the 1st Meeting of the ASEAN Regional Forum, Bangkok, 25 July. aseanregionalforum.asean.org/library/arf-chairmans-statements-and-reports.html?id=131.

(1996). Summary Report of the ARF Inter-Sessional Meeting on Confidence Building Measures, Tokyo, 18–19 January, and Jakarta, 15–16 April. aseanregionalforum.asean.org/files/library/ARF%20Chairman's%20Statements%20and%20Reports/The%20Third%20ASEAN%20Regional%20Forum,%201995–1996/ISG%20CBMs.doc.

(2014). *ASEAN Regional Forum at Twenty: Promoting Peace and Security in the Asia-Pacific*. aseanregionalforum.asean.org/files/ARF-Publication/A%20Commemorative%20Publication%20for%20the%2020th%20ASEAN%20Regional%20Forum.pdf.

(2016). Opening Ceremony, 28th and 29th ASEAN Summits and Related Summits, 6 September, Vientiane, Laos. www.flickr.com/photos/aseansecretariat/sets/72157672437484212/.

Associated Press. (2016). Malaysia PM urges world to act against 'genocide' of Myanmar's Rohingya. *The Guardian*, 4 December.

Ba, Alice. (2009). *(Re)Negotiating East and Southeast Asia: Region, Regionalism, and the Association of Southeast Asian Nations*, Stanford, CA: Stanford University Press.

Bandung Conference. (1955). Final communiqué of the Asian-African conference of Bandung (24 April). In Indonesian Ministry of Foreign Affairs, ed., *Asia-Africa Speak from Bandung*, Jakarta: Indonesian Ministry of Foreign Affairs, pp. 161–9.

Bauer, Joanne R. & Bell, Daniel A. eds. (1999). *The East Asian Challenge for Human Rights*, Cambridge: Cambridge University Press.

Bell, Daniel A. (2000). *East Meets West: Human Rights and Democracy in East Asia*, Princeton, NJ: Princeton University Press.

Buszynski, Leszek. (1998). Thailand and Myanmar: The perils of 'constructive engagement'. *Pacific Review*, **11**(2), 290–305. doi:10.1080/09512749808719258.

Caballero-Anthony, Mely. (1998). Mechanisms of dispute settlement: The ASEAN experience. *Contemporary Southeast Asia*, **20**(1), 38–66.

(2008). The ASEAN Charter: An opportunity missed or one that *cannot* be missed? *Southeast Asian Affairs 2008*, 71–85.

Castro, Amado. (1982). ASEAN economic co-operation. In Alison Broinowski, ed., *Understanding ASEAN*, New York: St. Martin's Press, pp. 70–91.

Cerulo, Karen A. (1995). *Identity Designs: The Sights and Sounds of a Nation*, New Brunswick, NJ: Rutgers University Press.

Chapman, Terrence L. (2009). Audience beliefs and international organization legitimacy. *International Organization*, **63**(4), 733–64. doi:10.1017/S0020818309990154.

Charlesworth, Hilary. (2010). Swimming to Cambodia: Justice and ritual in human rights after conflict. *Australian Yearbook of International Law*, **29**, 1–16.

Charlesworth, Hilary & Larking, Emma. (2014). Introduction: The regulatory power of the Universal Periodic Review. In Hilary Charlesworth and Emma Larking, eds., *Human Rights and the Universal Periodic Review: Rituals and Ritualism*, Cambridge: Cambridge University Press, pp. 1–21.

Chase, Oscar G. (2005). *Law, Culture, and Ritual: Disputing Systems in Cross-Cultural Context*, New York: New York University Press.

Chatterjee, Srikanta. (1990). ASEAN economic cooperation in the 1980s and 1990s. In Alison Broinowski, ed., *ASEAN into the 1990s*, Basingstoke: Macmillan Press, pp. 58–82.

Cheesman, Nick. (2017). How in Myanmar 'national races' came to surpass citizenship and exclude Rohingya. *Journal of Contemporary Asia*, **47**(3), 461–83. doi:10.1080/00472336.2017.1297476.

Colbert, Evelyn. (1986). ASEAN as a regional organization: Economics, politics, and security. In Karl D. Jackson, Sukhumbhand Paribatra and J.

Soedjati Djiwandono, eds., *ASEAN in Regional and Global Context*, Berkeley, CA: Institute of East Asian Studies, University of California, pp. 194–210.

Collins, Alan. (2007). Forming a security community: Lessons from ASEAN. *International Relations of the Asia-Pacific*, **7**(2), 203–25. doi:10.1093/irap/lcl007.

(2008). A people-oriented ASEAN: A door ajar or closed for civil society organizations? *Contemporary Southeast Asia*, **30**(2), 313–31.

Cook, Malcolm & Bisley, Nick. (2016). Contested Asia and the East Asia Summit. *Perspective*, 18 August. Singapore: ISEAS–Yusof Ishak Institute.

Creak, Simon. (2010). Sport and the theatrics of power in a postcolonial state: The National Games of 1960s Laos. *Asian Studies Review*, **34**(2), 191–210. doi:10.1080/10357821003802011.

(2017). Eternal friends and erstwhile enemies: The regional sporting community of the Southeast Asian games. *TRaNS: Trans-Regional and -National Studies of Southeast Asia*, **5**(1), 147–72. doi:10.1017/trn.2016.29.

Cribb, Robert. (2018). Southeast Asia: Historical context. In Alice Ba and Mark Beeson, eds, *Contemporary Southeast Asia: The Politics of Change, Contestation, and Adaptation*, London: Palgrave, pp. 17–33.

Croissant, Aurel. (2004). From transition to defective democracy: Mapping Asian democratization. *Democratization*, **11**(5), 156–78. doi:10.1080/13510340412331304633.

Davies, Mathew. (2012).The perils of incoherence: ASEAN, Myanmar and the avoidable failures of human rights socialization? *Contemporary Southeast Asia*, **34**(1), 1–22.

(2013a). ASEAN and human rights norms: Constructivism, rational choice, and the action-identity gap. *International Relations of the Asia-Pacific*, **13**(2), 207–31. doi:10.1093/irap/lct002.

(2013b). Explaining the Vientiane Action Programme: ASEAN and the institutionalisation of human rights. *Pacific Review*, **26**(3), 385–406. doi:10.1080/09512748.2013.788066.

(2014a). An agreement to disagree: The ASEAN Human Rights Declaration and the absence of regional identity in Southeast Asia. *Journal of Current Southeast Asian Affairs*, **33**(3), 107–29.

(2014b). *Realising Rights: How Regional Organisations Socialise Human Rights*, Abingdon: Routledge.

(2016). A community of practice: Explaining change and continuity in ASEAN's diplomatic environment. *Pacific Review*, **29**(2), 211–33. doi:10.1080/09512748.2015.1013495.

(2017). Important but de-centred: ASEAN's role in the Southeast Asian human rights space. *TRaNS: Trans-Regional and -National Studies of Southeast Asia*, **5**(1), 99–119. doi:10.1017/trn.2016.27.

(2018). Regional organisations and enduring defective democratic members. *Review of International Studies*, **44**(1), 174–91. doi:10.1017/ S0260210517000365.

Deutsch, Karl W. (1957). *Political Community and the North Atlantic Area: International Organization in the Light of Historical Experience*, Princeton, NJ: Princeton University Press.

Dosch, Jörn. (2017). The ASEAN economic community: Deep integration or just political window dressing? *TRaNS: Trans-Regional and -National Studies of Southeast Asia*, **5**(1), 25–47. doi:10.1017/trn.2016.28.

Eaton, Sarah & Stubbs, Richard. (2006). Is ASEAN powerful? Neo-realist versus constructivist approaches to power in Southeast Asia. *Pacific Review*, **19**(2), 135–55. doi:10.1080/09512740500473148.

Emmers, Ralf & See Seng Tan. (2012). The ASEAN Regional Forum and preventive diplomacy: A review essay. In Ralf Emmers, ed., *ASEAN and the Institutionalization of East Asia*, Abingdon: Routledge, pp. 89–102.

Emmerson, Donald K. (2006). Shocks of recognition: Leifer, realism, and regionalism in Southeast Asia. In Joseph Chinyong Liow and Ralf Emmers, eds., *Order and Security in Southeast Asia: Essays in Memory of Michael Leifer*, Abingdon: Routledge, pp. 10–28.

(2008). ASEAN's 'black swans'. *Journal of Democracy*, **19**(3), 70–84. doi:10.1353/jod.0.0014.

Faizullaev, Alisher. (2013). Diplomacy and symbolism. *The Hague Journal of Diplomacy*, **8**(2), 91–114. doi:10.1163/1871191X-12341254.

Finnemore, Martha & Sikkink, Kathryn. (1998). International norm dynamics and political change. *International Organization*, **52**(4), 887–917.

(2001). Taking stock: The constructivist research program in international relations and comparative politics. *Annual Review of Political Science*, **4**, 391–416.

Florini, Ann. (1996). The evolution of international norms. *International Studies Quarterly*, **40**(3), 363–89. doi:10.2307/2600716.

Frost, Frank. (1990). Introduction: ASEAN since 1967 – Origins, evolutions and recent developments. In Alison Broinowski, ed., *ASEAN into the 1990s*, Basingstoke: Macmillan Press, pp. 1–31.

Geertz, Clifford. (1980). *Negara: The Theatre State in Ninteenth-Century Bali*, Princeton, NJ: Princeton University Press.

Gerard, Kelly. (2014). ASEAN and civil society activities in 'created spaces': The limits of liberty. *Pacific Review*, **27**(2), 265–87. doi:10.1080/09512748.2014.882395.

 (2015). Explaining ASEAN's engagement of civil society in policy-making: Smoke and mirrors. *Globalizations*, **12**(3), 365–82. doi:10.1080/14747731.2015.1016304.

Goh, Evelyn. (2018). ASEAN-led multilateralism and regional order: The great power bargain deficit. In Gilbert Rozman and Joseph Chinyong Liow, eds, *International Relations and Asia's Southern Tier: ASEAN, Australia, and India*, Singapore: ASAN Institute for Policy Studies and Palgrave Macmillan, pp. 45–61.

Goldstein, Morris. (1998). The Asian financial crisis: Causes, cures, and systemic implications, Washington, DC: Institute for International Economics.

Gonzalez-Manalo, Rosario. (2009). Drafting ASEAN's tomorrow: The Eminent Persons Group and the ASEAN Charter. In Tommy Koh, Rosario G. Manalo and Walter Woon, eds., *The Making of the ASEAN Charter*, Singapore: World Scientific Publishing, pp. 37–46.

Haacke, Jürgen. (1999). The concept of flexible engagement and the practice of enhanced interaction: Intramural challenges to the 'ASEAN way'. *Pacific Review*, **12**(4), 581–611. doi:10.1080/09512749908719307.

 (2005). *ASEAN's Diplomatic and Security Culture: Origins, Development and Prospects*, Abingdon: Routledge.

Hadi, Umar. (2006). Human rights promotion in the ASEAN Security Community: An overview. Paper presented at the AICOHR–ASEAN–ISIS Colloquium on Human Rights, Manila, 15–16 May.

Human Rights Watch. (2012). Civil society denounces adoption of flawed ASEAN Human Rights Declaration. 19 November. www.hrw.org/news/2012/11/19/civil-society-denounces-adoption-flawed-asean-human-rights-declaration.

Hurd, Ian. (2002). Legitimacy, power, and the symbolic life of the UN Security Council. *Global Governance*, **8**(1), 35–51.

 (2005). The strategic use of liberal internationalism: Libya and the UN sanctions, 1992–2003. *International Organization*, **59**(3), 495–526. doi:10.1017/S0020818305050186.

Irvine, Roger. (1982). The formative years of ASEAN, 1967–1975. In Alison Broinowski, ed., *Understanding ASEAN*, New York: St. Martin's Press, pp. 8–36.

Johnston, Alastair I. (1999). The myth of the ASEAN way? Explaining the evolution of the ASEAN Regional Forum. In Helga Haftendom, Robert O. Keohane and Celeste A. Wallander, eds, *Imperfect Unions: Security Institutions over Time and Space*, Oxford: Oxford University Press, pp. 287–324.

Jones, David Martin. (2008). Security and democracy: The ASEAN Charter and the dilemmas of regionalism in South-East Asia. *International Affairs*, **84**(4), 735–56. doi:10.1111/j.1468-2346.2008.00735.x.

Jones, David Martin & Smith, Michael L. R. (2002). ASEAN's imitation community. *Orbis*, **46**(1), 93–109.

(2006). *ASEAN and East Asian International Relations: Regional Delusion*, Cheltenham: Edward Elgar Publishing.

Jones, Lee. (2008). ASEAN's albatross: ASEAN's Burma policy, from constructive engagement to critical disengagement. *Asian Security*, **4**(3), 271–93. doi:10.1080/14799850802306484.

(2012). *ASEAN, Sovereignty and Intervention in Southeast Asia*, Basingstoke: Palgrave Macmillan.

(2016). Explaining the failure of the ASEAN economic community: The primacy of domestic political economy. *Pacific Review*, **29**(5), 647–70. doi:10.1080/09512748.2015.1022593.

Kahler, Miles. (2000). Legalization as strategy: The Asia-Pacific case. *International Organization*, **54**(3), 549–71.

Katsumata, Hiro. (2004). Why is ASEAN diplomacy changing? From 'non-interference' to 'open and frank discussions'. *Asian Survey*, **44**(2), 237–54. doi:10.1525/as.2004.44.2.237.

(2006). Establishment of the ASEAN Regional Forum: Constructing a 'talking shop' or a 'norm brewery'? *Pacific Review* **19**(2), 181–98. doi:10.1080/09512740500473197.

Kaufmann, Chaim D. & Pape, Robert A. (1999). Explaining costly international moral action: Britain's sixty-year campaign against the Atlantic slave trade. *International Organization*, **53** (4),631–68.

Kausikan, Bilahari. (2017). ASEAN's greatest challenges lie within grouping. Today Online, 3 October. www.todayonline.com/world/aseans-greatest-challenges-lie-within-grouping-bilahari?cid=todayfbcommented.

Keesing, Roger M. (2012). On not understanding symbols: Toward an anthropology of incomprehension. *HAU: Journal of Ethnographic Theory*, **2**(2), 406–30. doi.org/10.14318/hau2.2.023.

Kertzer, David I. (1988). *Rituals, Politics and Power*, New Haven, CT: Yale University Press.

Kim, Min-hyung. (2018). East Asian international relations and international relations theory: Where does a poor fit exist, and what to do about it? *Journal of Asian and African Studies* doi:10.1177/0021909618777269.

Kraft, Herman Joseph S. (2001). Human rights, ASEAN and constructivism: Revisiting the 'Asian values' discourse. *Philippine Political Science Journal*, **22**(45), 33–54. doi:10.1080/01154451.2001.9754224.

Kratochwil, Friedrich V. (1989). *Rules, Norms, and Decisions: On the Conditions of Practical and Legal Reasoning in International Relations and Domestic Affairs*, Cambridge: Cambridge University Press.

Larking, Emma. (2017). Human rights rituals: Masking neoliberalism and inequality, and marginalizing alternative world views. *Canadian Journal of Law and Society*, **32**(1), 1–18. doi:10.1017/cls.2017.3.

Larkins, Jeremy. (1994). Representations, symbols, and social facts: Durkheim and IR theory. *Millennium: Journal of International Studies*, **23**(2), 239–64.

Leifer, Michael. (1974). Regional order in South-East Asia: An uncertain prospect. *The Round Table*, **64**(255), 309–17.

(1989). *ASEAN and the Security of South-East Asia*. Abingdon: Routledge.

Leviter, Lee. (2010). The ASEAN Charter: ASEAN failure or member failure. *New York University Journal of International Law and Politics*, **43**(1), 159–210.

MacIntyre, Andrew J. (2003). *The Power of Institutions: Political Architecture and Governance*, Ithaca, NY: Cornell University Press.

Malik, Mohan. (2006). The East Asia Summit. *Australian Journal of International Affairs*, **60**(2), 207–11. doi:10.1080/10357710600696134.

Mansfield, Edward D. & Pevehouse, Jon C. (2006). Democratization and international organizations. *International Organization*, **60** (1),137–67.

Merkel, Wolfgang. (2004). Embedded and defective democracies. *Democratization*, **11**(5), 33–58. doi:10.1080/13510340412331304598.

Möller, Kay. (1998). Cambodia and Burma: The ASEAN way ends here. *Asian Survey*, **38**(12), 1087–104. doi:10.2307/2645823.

Moore, Sally Falk & Myerhoff, Barbara G. (1977). Introduction: Secular ritual: Forms and meanings. In Sally Falk Moore and Barbara G. Myerhoff, eds., *Secular Ritual*, Assen: Uitgeverij Van Gorcum, pp. 3–24.

Morada, Noel M. (2008). ASEAN at 40: Prospects for community building in Southeast Asia. *Asia-Pacific Review*, **15**(1), 36–55. doi:10.1080/13439000802134043.

Morlino, Leonardo. (2004). What is a 'good' democracy? *Democratization*, **11**(5), 10–32. doi:10.1080/13510340412331304589.

Muntarbhorn, Vitit. (1986). *The Challenge of Law: Legal Cooperation among ASEAN Countries*, Bangkok: Institute of Security and International Studies.

Narine, Shaun. (1997). ASEAN and the ARF: The limits of the 'ASEAN way'. *Asian Survey*, **37**(10), 961–78.

(2009). ASEAN in the twenty-first century: A sceptical review. *Cambridge Review of International Affairs*, **22**(3), 369–86. doi:10.1080/09557570903104065.

Ness, Gayl D. (1962). Letter to Mr. Richard H. Nolte, 1 May. www.icwa.org/wp-content/uploads/2015/09/GDN-14.pdf.

Neumann, Iver B. (2011). Euro-centric diplomacy: Challenging but manageable. *European Journal of International Relations*, **18**(2), 299–321. doi:10.1177/1354066110389831.

Nischalke, Tobias Ingo. (2000). Insights from ASEAN's foreign policy cooperation: The 'ASEAN way', a real spirit or a phantom? *Contemporary Southeast Asia*, **22**(1), 89–112.

Ong Keng Yong. (2004). Civil society and regional cooperation. Speech delivered at the 31st International Council on Social Welfare, Kuala Lumpur, 18 August.

Onuf, Nicholas Greenwood. (1989). *World of Our Making: Rules and Rule in Social Theory and International Relations*, Columbia, SC: University of South Carolina Press.

Oren, Ido & Solomon, Ty. (2015). WMD, WMD, WMD: Securitisation through ritualised incantation of ambiguous phrases. *Review of International Studies*, **41** (2),313–36. doi:10.1017/S0260210514000205.

Parameswaran, Prashanth. (2016). Assessing ASEAN's South China Sea position in its post-ruling statement. *The Diplomat*, 25 July. thediplomat.com/2016/07/assessing-aseans-south-china-sea-position-in-its-post-ruling-statement/.

Pereira, Derwin. (2007). Straits Times' interview with Singapore Foreign Minister George Yeo, 2–3 October. www.mfa.gov.sg/content/mfa/overseasmission/washington/newsroom/press_statements/2007/200710/press_200710_08.html.

Pevehouse, Jon C. (2002). Democracy from the outside-in? International organizations and democratization. *International Organization*, **56**(3), 515–49.

Phillips, Andrew. (2017). Contesting the Confucian peace: Civilization, barbarism and international hierarchy in East Asia. *European Journal of International Relations*, online, 1–25. doi:1354066117716265.

Pisanò, Attilio. (2014). Human rights and sovereignty in the ASEAN path towards a human rights declaration. *Human Rights Review*, **15**(4), 399–411. doi:10.1007/s12142-014-0313-7.

Pitsuwan, Surin. (1998). Currency turmoil in Asia: The strategic impact. Remarks at the 12th Asia-Pacific Roundtable, Kuala Lumpur, 1 June.

(2013). Speech by outgoing Secretary-General (2008–2012). Ceremony for the transfer of office of the Secretary–General of ASEAN, Jakarta, 9 January. asean.org/?static_post=speech-by-outgoing-secretary-general-2008-2012-he-surin-pitsuwan-ceremony-for-the-transfer-of-office-of-the-secretary-general-of-asean-3.

Pollard, Vincent K. (1970). ASA and ASEAN, 1961–1967: Southeast Asian regionalism. *Asian Survey*, **10**(3), 244–55.

Price, Richard & Reus-Smit, Christian. (1998). Dangerous liaisons? Critical international theory and constructivism. *European Journal of International Relations*, **4**(3), 259–94.

Radelet, Steven & Sachs, Jeffrey. (1998). The onset of the East Asian financial crisis. NBER Working Paper 6680, Cambridge, MA: National Bureau of Economic Research.

Ravenhill, John. (2009). East Asian regionalism: Much ado about nothing? *Review of International Studies*, **35**(S1), 215–35. doi:10.1017/S0260210509008493.

Renshaw, Catherine Shanahan. (2013). The ASEAN Human Rights Declaration 2012. *Human Rights Law Review*, **13**(3), 557–79. doi:10.1093/hrlr/ngt016.

Risse, Thomas, Ropp, Stephen C. & Sikkink, Kathryn eds. (1999). *The Power of Human Rights: International Norms and Domestic Change*, Cambridge: Cambridge University Press.

(2013). *The Persistent Power of Human Rights: From Commitment to Compliance*, Cambridge: Cambridge University Press.

Roberts, Christopher B. (2012). *ASEAN Regionalism: Cooperation, Values and Institutionalisation*, Abingdon: Routledge.

Rubinstein, Robert A. (2005). Intervention and culture: An anthropological approach to peace operations. *Security Dialogue*, **36**(4), 527–44. doi:10.1177/0967010605060454.

Rüland, Jürgen. (2000). ASEAN and the Asian crisis: Theoretical implications and practical consequences for Southeast Asian regionalism. *Pacific Review*, **13**(3), 421–51. doi:10.1080/09512740050147942.

(2009). Deepening ASEAN cooperation through democratization? The Indonesian legislature and foreign policymaking. *International Relations of the Asia-Pacific*, **9**(3), 373–402. doi:10.1093/irap/lcp010.

Schirch, Lisa. (2005). *Ritual and Symbol in Peacebuilding*, West Hartford, CT: Kumarian Press.

Sending, Ole Jacob, Pouliot, Vincent & Neumann, Iver B., eds. (2015). *Diplomacy and the Making of World Politics*, Cambridge: Cambridge University Press.

Sennett, Richard. (2013). *Together: The Rituals, Pleasures and Politics of Cooperation*, London: Penguin.

Severino, Rodolfo C. (2000). Sovereignty, intervention and the ASEAN way. Address to the ASEAN Scholars' Roundtable, Singapore Institute of International Affairs, 3 July. asean.org/?static_post=sovereignty-interven tion-and-the-asean-way-3-july-2000.

Singapore Government. (1986). Joint statement by five ASEAN countries on the Philippines. Press Release, 23 February. www.nas.gov.sg/archiveson line/data/pdfdoc/372–1986-02–23.pdf.

Stubbs, Richard. (2008). The ASEAN alternative? Ideas, institutions and the challenge to 'global' governance. *Pacific Review*, **21**(4), 451–68. doi:10.1080/09512740802294713.

Sukma, Rizal. (2011). Indonesia finds a new voice. *Journal of Democracy*, **22**(4), 110–23. doi:10.1353/jod.2011.0057.

TalkVietnam. (2010). ASEAN welcomes Myanmar's general elections, 9 November. www.talkvietnam.com/2010/11/asean-welcomes-myanmars-general-elections/.

Tan, Hsien-Li. (2011). *The ASEAN Intergovernmental Commission on Human Rights: Institutionalising Human Rights in Southeast Asia*, Cambridge: Cambridge University Press.

Tay, Simon S. C. (2008). The ASEAN Charter: Between national sovereignty and the region's constitutional moment. *Singapore Year Book of International Law*, **12**, 151–70.

Thayer, Carlyle A. (1990). ASEAN and Indochina: The dialogue. In Alison Broinowski, ed., *ASEAN into the 1990s*, Basingstoke: Macmillan Press, pp. 138–61.

United Nations. (1963). Manila Accord between the Philippines, the Federation of Malaya and Indonesia, 31 July. treaties.un.org/doc/Publication/UNTS/Volume%20550/volume-550-I-8029-English.pdf.

(2010). Secretary-General says Myanmar authorities need to demonstrate credibility of elections, urges immediate release of remaining political prisoners, SG/SM/13238, New York, 8 November. www.un.org/press/en/2010/sgsm13238.doc.htm.

Walzer, Michael. (1967). On the role of symbolism in political thought. *Political Science Quarterly*, **82**(2), 191–204. doi:10.2307/2147214.

Wendt, Alexander. (1999). *Social Theory of International Politics*, Cambridge: Cambridge University Press.

White III, George O. (2000). From snowplows to Siopao – Trying to compete in a global marketplace: The ASEAN free trade area. *Tulsa Journal of Comparative and International Law*, **8**(1), 177–99.

Yukawa, Taku. (2017). The ASEAN way as a symbol: An analysis of discourses on the ASEAN norms. Pacific Review, 4 September, online, 1–17. doi:10.1080/09512748.2017.1371211.

Cambridge Elements $\equiv$

Politics and Society in Southeast Asia

Edward Aspinall
Australian National University
Edward Aspinall is a professor of politics at the Coral Bell School
of Asia-Pacific Affairs, Australian National University. A specialist of Southeast
Asia, especially Indonesia, much of his research has focused on democratisation,
ethnic politics and civil society in Indonesia and, most recently, clientelism
across Southeast Asia.

Meredith L. Weiss
University at Albany, SUNY
Meredith L. Weiss is Professor of Political Science at the University at Albany,
SUNY. Her research addresses political mobilization and contention, the
politics of identity and development, and electoral politics in Southeast Asia,
with particular focus on Malaysia and Singapore.

About the Series
The Elements series Politics and Society in Southeast Asia includes
both country-specific and thematic studies on one of the world's most dynamic
regions. Each title, written by a leading scholar of that country or theme,
combines a succinct, comprehensive, up-to-date overview of debates
in the scholarly literature with original analysis and a clear argument.

Cambridge Elements ≡

Politics and Society in Southeast Asia

Elements in the Series

Printed in the United States
By Bookmasters